The Russian Odyssey

ROY DEWS

abbott press

Abbott Press books may be ordered through booksellers or by contacting:

Abbott Press
1663 Liberty Drive
Bloomington, IN 47403
www.abbottpress.com
Phone: 1 (866) 697-5310

ISBN: 978-1-4582-1964-0 (sc)
ISBN: 978-1-4582-1965-7 (hc)
ISBN: 978-1-4582-1966-4 (e)

Library of Congress Control Number: 2015918847

Print information available on the last page.

Abbott Press rev. date: 01/19/2016

From The Authors Daughter

I chose to publish this book that my father so beautifully wrote. His words depict the man he was, which was very fond of people and life in general. He always went the extra mile. I am so very proud of this book and my father being able to do such a good job while writing it on a very busy trip and being 66 years old at the time. This was a very challenging trip and my father was no "spring chicken" so to speak when he and his brother in law took the trip.

I decided to publish this book and started working on doing so in 2013 and had planned to present it to my father for Father's Day 2014. Unfortunately he passed away 1 month earlier on May 19 2014 after many years battling Parkinson's disease.

I wanted to do something for my father as he had done so many things for so many people throughout his life. My father surprised me with a horse one Christmas. I awoke and looked in our backyard and to my surprise there was a horse adorned with a large red bow. It was special things like this that I will always hold in my heart. My father was a great provider and worked very hard to give us the things that we needed and wanted. We spoke many times about my sister and our childhood days and he would smile and say... **"The Best Days of My Life"**! He meant every word of it, I could feel and see it.

So Dad, here is your book. I am so sorry it did not make it on time but it is here now for the world to enjoy.

I love you dad... and Thanks for being **"The Best Dad a Girl Could Ever Have!"**

More about the author:

Richard Roy Dews was born in 1927 and grew up in Lynchburg, Virginia. His first job was delivering for a pharmacy. He rode a motorcycle to do this and this started a love affair with this mode of transportation. He and his best friend made a trip to Canada, riding together on one. All of his life he talked about wanting a motorcycle.

When he was 17, being very patriotic, he decided to join the Navy. This was in the midst of World War II. He served a year and the war was over. He came home wondering what he was going to do. A friend told him he was going to Phillips Business College and Roy decided that would be a good thing for him to do also and the GI Bill would pay for it. This turned out to be a very fortunate choice for him. Not only did he study Accounting, Economics, Business English, etc. but also learned shorthand and typing, excelling in both. He completed the two year course.

Then his old friend, the pharmacist, told him that NCR Corporation (then National Cash Register) had advertised a job opening for an office manager and encouraged him to apply for it. At first he did not feel qualified for the job and hesitated to apply, but the pharmacist went to the NCR Branch Manager and told him he would be crazy not to hire Roy because he was very qualified and also "the best boy in Lynchburg". He was hired and this began a life-long career with this company. After a few years as Office Manager, he was encouraged to go into sales. Another time he hesitated but decided to take a Dale Carnegie course to bolster his salesmanship, and hence another type of career. After several years of sales, he became a Branch Manager, moving many times to new locations while moving up the corporate ladder with his first wife Shirley, daughters Jane and Susan. He was promoted to Regional Marketing Director of the Southeastern region of the U.S and ended up residing in Atlanta for the past 40 plus years. Many men attribute their success to his early training in discipline, organization, integrity, and even dress.

After retiring he and his wife Marie spent a great deal of time traveling. They drove through France, Germany, Switzerland, Austria, Spain; visited China, Japan, Hawaii, Alaska, most of Canada, Mexico, South America, and made a driving trip through the United States which culminated in their having been in all 50 states. Then there was the trip that he wrote about in this book.

Roy's only two children Jane and Susan are still living.

Clarence "Andy" Anderson

Andy grew up on a small farm near Ellijay, GA. He spent three years in the Navy, serving in the Pacific arena, during World War II. When he came out he decided he wanted to establish a jewelry store in nearby Blue Ridge, GA and decided to use his GI Bill to go to a trade school instead of college. He became quite a legend in Blue Ridge. He would let young men buy their wedding rings from him with only small payments each month. This, plus his warm and engaging personality, helped him to develop the small store into a very successful business. He later opened a store in Ellijay. He was also very active in his church and politically active, although not running for an elective office. He was a born leader in his extended family and in every part of his life.

Andy always took time to enjoy life and one of his favorite things was traveling. When his two sons were young, the three of them would take off to Canada, Alaska, and other parts of the world. He continued to travel the world and after this trip to Russia he came home and went to China and also Peru very soon afterwards. Unfortunately this was probably a little too much activity so close together and he suffered a stroke from which he never completely recovered.

Preface

Roy Dews

I wrote this book about our fifty-two-day trip because of my wife's request for a diary. I wrote it without research and almost without references. Certain facts may not be completely correct, and all opinions are those of the writer.

Introduction

Russia and the Trans-Siberian Railroad have been a great interest of mine for many years. Andy Anderson, my brother-in-law, told me he also was very interested in this area of the world. In February 1993, we began to make plans for this trip and decided on a departure date of June 7, 1993; we wanted to travel during reasonably warm weather in that area.

Utilizing my frequent flyer miles on Delta, we planned to begin the trip in Warsaw via Frankfurt, making side trips to the Baltic countries of Lithuania, Latvia, and Estonia; to Finland, since Helsinki was across the Baltic Sea and the Gulf of Finland; and on to St. Petersburg, Russia, also on the Gulf of Finland.

From St. Petersburg, we planned to travel to Moscow and take the Trans-Siberian with layover stops in Russian cities recommended by a travel agency, including Ekaterinburg and Omsk, which had previously been cities closed to foreigners. Russian residents of these strategic military cities were also kept from visiting foreign countries.

Another stopover was to be Irkutsk, with a visit to Lake Baikal, the deepest lake in the world; it holds one-sixth of the world's freshwater supply. From Irkutsk, we wanted to travel to Ulan Bator in Mongolia. This proved difficult since travel agencies were inexperienced with arranging travel in that part of the world.

We learned we couldn't make a double entry back into Russia, but we persisted, and our local agent, Prestige Travel, canceled its involvement with the out-of-town travel agent with whom it had been working and contacted Rahim Travel, in Lake Worth, Florida, which secured the double-entry visa back into Russia with ease.

We were to go from Irkutsk east about 200 miles to Ulan Ude and then south to Ulan Bator, Mongolia, a two-night train ride. We planned to return to Ulan Ude for a one-night stay. Another two-night train ride would take us to Khabarovsk, about 5,500 miles east of Moscow.

Vladivostok, the Soviet Union's naval port on the Pacific, had been closed to foreigners until about a year before our trip, and the travel agent told us we wouldn't be able to visit that city. Evidently, travel agents in general didn't know it was then open since the Soviet Union was no longer in existence. Prestige Travel was persistent, so we were able to visit Vladivostok and conclude our 5,810-mile Trans-Siberian trip, the entire length of the Trans-Siberian, which was our goal. From Vladivostok, the Russian airline Aeroflot was to take us back to Moscow for a night and a day.

Andy suggested we go through Beijing, China. However, that was supposed to be impossible, and I gave up on it far too easily. Further persistence would have allowed us to travel by train from Vladivostok to Beijing, continue north through southern Mongolia to Ulan Bator and Irkutsk, and return to Moscow without retracing our path and without additional expense. Also, traveling that part of Asia would have been a real bonus.

Having an interest in the southern part of the former Soviet Union, we decided to go to Odessa on the Black Sea after our return to Moscow, which was supposedly the base for the Soviet Black Sea fleet but is now a part of Ukraine. We later learned that the controversial fleet, the ownership of which Ukraine and Russia contested, was actually based in Sevastopol, also in Ukraine, but not a reasonable trip for us.

The trip from Moscow to Odessa was a 700-mile train ride through a rich agricultural area, which was formerly called the breadbasket of the Soviet Union, and to warmer weather on the Black Sea.

We had thought we could go from Odessa to Kiev or to Bucharest, Romania, or some other place since we thought we would have a five-day free period. That turned out to be only two free days, and we spent those in Odessa.

Our final visit was to be Istanbul, an old city split by the Straits of Bosporus in the Dardanelles; a small western part is in continental Europe while the much larger eastern area is in continental Asia; it's the only city in both continents. The Dardanelles link the Black Sea and the Mediterranean; that would allow a visit to another warmer country and one of Middle Eastern culture and atmosphere, a different part of the world.

On July 29, 1993, fifty-two days after the beginning of our trip, our flight from Istanbul to Atlanta via Frankfurt would end our Russian odyssey.

Our Russian Odyssey

Our Russian trip began in Atlanta on June 7, 1993. We departed at 7:40 p.m., bound for Frankfurt and then to Warsaw, Poland. Andy Anderson and I began our fifty-two-day journey with the understanding that the Russian part was probably not for vacationers but for those who seek some adventure. Perhaps adventure had more of an allure for Andy that I did.

After a one-and-three-quarters' hour flight from Frankfurt to Warsaw and a three-night stay, there, we planned to fly to Vilnius, Lithuania, for one night and take an overnight train to Riga, Latvia. The following night we planned to take a train to Tallinn, Estonia, for one night.

After a day and night in Tallinn, we were to take a day ferry to Helsinki for three nights and a train to St. Petersburg for five nights. We planned to fly from there on Aeroflot to Moscow for a four-night stay before boarding the Trans-Siberian. Beginning in Moscow, the Trans-Siberian travels a distance of 5810 miles to Vladivostok. Fortunately, on the way we will make several stops—one in Omsk for two nights, another in Ekaterinburg for two nights, the next in Irkutsk for two nights, and will include a trip to Lake Baikal.

From Irkutsk, we planned to take a two-night train ride to Ulan Bator in Mongolia for three nights. After Ulan Bator, we would travel back in a northeasterly direction to Ulan Ude, which appears to be about 200 miles from the point at which we left the Trans-Siberian to go into Mongolia. From Ulan Ude, where we planned to spend one night, we wanted to travel to Khabarovsk for a two-night stay. The next stop would be for two nights in Vladivostok.

The conclusion of our Trans-Siberian trip would be an Aeroflot flight from Vladivostok to Moscow for one night. We would proceed to Odessa, Ukraine, on the Black Sea for two nights, and the next five days would be free. We weren't certain whether we would go to Kiev or some other place before proceeding to Istanbul.

In an attempt to eliminate a $700 one-way flight for each of us from Kiev to Istanbul, we took a chance on getting there some other way. Perhaps we would end up in Bucharest, Romania, and take a train to Istanbul.

We planned to visit Istanbul for three nights before returning to Atlanta.

Andy and I knew our trip was not going to be completely fun, but as the books say, more of an adventure. We didn't know what adventures we would have and how much fun we would have. It would be something we very much wanted to do, however.

Warsaw—June 8, 1993

We arrived in Warsaw. After having been up for more than twenty-four hours, we took a nap for an hour or so and got up about three in the afternoon. We took a four-hour city tour the next day.

Warsaw wasn't beautiful; it was dull and gray. Its desolation and destruction began in September 1939, when Hitler invaded Poland and started World War II. In late 1944, when the city was still occupied by the Nazis, the Warsaw revolt took place and destroyed much of the city as well as its inhabitants. The Poles rose up against the Germans, hoping they would be aided by the Russians, but the Russians had taken the outskirts of the city, called Praga, and simply waited for the Nazis to eliminate those who wanted freedom for Poland. The Nazis accomplished much of that before fleeing. Warsaw fell to the Russians.

We visited memorials to the Warsaw uprising in 1944. Of particular interest was a memorial to the Warsaw ghetto, an uprising that took place I believe in 1941; the residences of approximately 500,000 people were destroyed, and many lost their lives.

We saw the presidential palace, the building where the Warsaw Pact had been signed. The presidency was held at that time by Lech Walesa. He didn't live in the presidential palace; he preferred to travel between Warsaw and Gdansk, where his wife and family of eight children lived.

We took a taxi to Laizienkowski Park and spent a few hours there and at Wilanow Park. We found ourselves with no Polish currency to pay for the taxi ride back, and we couldn't find any place to exchange money as it was a Polish holy day—not even buses were running. We took taxi back to the hotel, chancing that we could exchange some money there, which we did. The cost of the taxi trips was about the same as it would have been in the United States—$22 or so for that day.

Both parks were beautiful but in need of manicures and maintenance; this we considered to be evidence of Poland's having been a Soviet satellite. Warsaw had many trees, and we had seen plenty of small agricultural plots when we flew into the country from Frankfurt. It seemed that so much agriculture would be able to feed the world, but the small garden plots we saw seemed to be infertile or not very productive even considering the fact that it was early in the season. We wondered if that was due to a lack of fertilizer.

Warsaw is a city of approximately 1.6 million with very plain and old buildings. It was evident that during the previous forty-plus years, communism had taken a huge toll on the infrastructure. Someone in Warsaw told us that the infrastructure had totally collapsed. We saw huge but very bleak and gray apartment complexes of typical Soviet construction—cheap and shoddy. We saw signs of entrepreneurs at work—capitalism at work, as I put it; some quality efforts were going into refurbishing businesses after years of Communist-era neglect.

I had always wanted to visit Auschwitz in Poland, but it was at least a day away, and we hadn't planned for it because it was too far away from any city served by Delta.

As we left Warsaw, I had the feeling we were beginning to see what it was like to live in a society that had deprived its people of incentives and motivation to do great things for themselves and their country.

Vilnius, Lithuania—June 11, 1993

We flew LOT, the major Polish airline, to Vilnius, a trip that took less than an hour. The two-engine jet was similar to a DC-9 but was a Soviet made plane; it had old-style seats and open bins for storage overhead. Service was very good; we ate a reasonable breakfast and had coffee, et cetera. Our stewardesses looked like typical Americans.

In Vilnius, we saw two people holding up a sign that read "Anderson and Dews"; they drove us to our hotel. Entry into the Baltic countries was very easy—no visas required—but I had to list in detail how much money, jewelry, and gold I had brought with me, and they seemed to be suspicious of me. Andy's honest face got him right through customs without question, however.

We checked into the Hotel Lietuva; our room was reasonably comfortable, something like a $50 Holiday Inn room in the States. We paid $93 for two people. As was the case with our hotel room in Warsaw, the rooms and bathrooms were very clean but equipped with extremely small bottles of shampoo and very small pieces of soap, evidence that material goods were expensive or not plentiful. However, we didn't notice any long lines anywhere of people queueing up for food or other items. We guessed that capitalism was at work making things available for those who had the money.

We arranged for a tour of Vilnius; Lira was our tour guide, and our driver had a car similar to a Ford Tempo, which wouldn't have been available in the country prior to its independence from the Soviet Union. We learned Vilnius had a population of about 500,000. It was clean and had beautiful parks and wide streets, much like Warsaw but without modern architecture.

In 1939 or 1940, Hitler made an agreement with Stalin that Russia could have the Baltic States, but in July 1941, Hitler attacked Russia and occupied the three Baltic States. The first thing our tour guide told us was that Stalin had relocated a million people to the north pole. Later, we figured out that he had meant Siberia, but perhaps "north pole" and "Siberia" were used interchangeably. It's said no one ever knew what happened to all those people. The Nazis occupied the Baltic States until late 1944, when they were recaptured by the Soviet Union.

We saw large churches that were closed or under restoration; this was evidence of communisms' atheism. I thought that due to the forty-plus years of Soviet control, it would take time for the people there, having been unable to practice their religion freely, to redevelop their association with churches and religion.

Poland has always been a very religious country—90 percent of its population is Catholic. Cardinal Wyszynski was imprisoned for several years because of his views that clashed with those of the Communists. We saw the place of his burial and either a monument or a place that had been dedicated to his memory. Poland's Solidarity union, headed by Lech Walesa, was the forerunner of the independence movements that rebelled against Soviet domination. When Poland started gaining some independence, such as when it became unionized, the thinking was that other Eastern-bloc countries would follow—domino style—in resisting the Soviet Union.

The second day in Vilnius, we found a rental car—$35 for ten hours with $10 extra for the driver. We weren't able to rent the car without the driver. It was a nice car, a General Motors Opel built in Germany, again, one that wouldn't have been available before the country's independence.

Our driver was supposed to know English, but he spoke only Lithuanian and French, so we couldn't communicate with him verbally. However, he was very good, and we enjoyed a day touring the countryside. On Saturday, we traveled 265 kilometers and paid 7¢ for each one—$18 for mileage on top of the rental and driver's fee. The countryside was very flat; we saw children and women wielding pitchforks to "pitch" hay onto wagons and trucks. Some women were in bathing suits. We could see that the hay had been cut by hand, most likely the way it had been cut for generations. That sight was one of the outstanding parts of our trip.

We visited an area where old log cabins and all kinds of devices, fixtures, and tools from perhaps a hundred years ago were being restored. The log cabins were impressive structures made of large timbers. Many of them had dirt floors, and Andy spotted many tools; some he recognized, while he had to figure out what others were for and how they worked. But they were all handmade tools—relics from the past of extremely good quality. Necessity is the mother of invention; we could tell they were all very functional. It reminded me that people are very much alike all around the world; they're motivated by the same needs, desires, and interests in spite of cultural differences.

The highlight of our visit, Kaunas, Lithuania, was a very big, beautiful church that had been built in 1471 but had been abandoned. A church next to it was being renovated and brought up to date, an indication that religion was on the move again.

We returned to Vilnius via Traikai to visit an old fort and an interesting little town people had recommended, but the old fort was closed. We bought some ice cream, which was tasty but not of the quality we were accustomed to. The people in this part of the world loved ice cream, and it was quite inexpensive.

Our guide told us that about 20 percent of the population in Lithuania was Russian. The Soviet Union had attempted to settle the Baltic States with as many Russians as possible to prevent the very thing that had happened a couple of years earlier. We saw evidence of Coca-Cola, Sprite, Marlboros, Snickers, and many other standard American products in Lithuania much as we had seen in Poland. But their quantities and the places we could buy such items weren't nearly as numerous as they were in the States. We had difficulties at times finding restaurants or stores to buy this or that; the signage we were used to in the States wasn't that common, and we took that as evidence that not much had been done to keep the infrastructure updated.

Our travel agent picked us up for an 11:20 p.m. train to Riga, Latvia, and dropped us off right at the car in which we were to sleep. That was a good thing; I don't think we would have been able to decipher the signs on our own. We were in a hard sleeper —four beds to a room. We knew from having read about it that there was no distinction made between male and female occupants in these cars. Andy and I had been assigned to different compartments; Andy was the lucky one; a good-looking woman in her twenties had been assigned to his compartment. But she talked Andy into having me trade rooms with her so Andy and I could share a compartment. That made me very happy. I didn't want Andy sleeping with a female if I wasn't going to.

We pulled our door together and tested it for security's sake. We couldn't get it open after we had locked it. We pushed and shoved and finally opened the door, relieved that we wouldn't be locked in if anything happened. We pushed the door together without locking them. We did drop a safety latch to keep the door closed. We felt reasonably secure with this safety latch.

About 5:00 a.m., we heard a banging on the door. Andy and I were very lucky. We welcomed two good-looking females in their twenties into our compartment. Andy and I were just as happy as we could be about that. We didn't believe Betty and Marie, Andy's and my wives respectively, would believe us. I said we would take pictures. The young women were evidently very experienced in traveling; they stepped on the table that was between the two bunk beds and climbed up very easily. The four of us tried to make ourselves comfortable and go to sleep again. Believe me—it was difficult to fall asleep with young women in our room.

A short while later, we heard a loud bang on our door. Our passports were being inspected. Andy found his passport but realized his billfold, in which he had about $200, was missing. I thought that it was the result of a pickpocket or that he had just misplaced it in the room. He had left his trousers at the foot of his bed toward the window away from the door with his billfold in them.

Shortly after, I realized my watch was missing. I'd put it on top of a blanket so I could see the time during the night. My pepper spray was gone too. It wasn't in clear view, but I had it in easy reach for protection. Andy's calculator was gone. We felt extremely fortunate that all our money, excessive cash in fact, hadn't been touched. Andy's money was in his belt in the same trousers from which the billfold was removed. My money, which I had in a billfold, a leg money belt, and a waist money belt, was untouched under the blanket. Perhaps we could write a book, *Theft on the Soviet Express.*

Riga, Latvia—Sunday, June 13, 1993

When we arrived in Riga, the next-door female—Andy's former roommate—met her husband, and he helped us find the travel agent who was supposed to pick us up and take us to Hotel Latvia.

Latvia, founded in 1201, has a population of about six million, and Riga has a population of 900,000. Approximately 66 percent of the population was Russian. The tour we took left us with the impression that the city was very much like Vilnius, only larger. The streets and highways in all the places we had visited that far on our trip were in very good shape. Riga has some wide streets and some very nice parks, but they were not manicured to show their real beauty. Riga's buildings were much like others we had seen; they showed evidence of lack of attention. We saw very few police officers and almost no military in any place we had been. We understood that the Russian army was still in the Baltic countries to an extent but would be removed in the near future.

We went on a tour to a beach on the Baltic, about twenty miles away. We saw an elderly gentleman and his young friend go for a swim on a day Andy and I were wearing jackets. The swimming season in this beach resort, Juranalai, began on June 15 and lasted through August, forty-five days. However, mid-June that year was certainly no swimming time; the water was very cold and the air was too chilly.

The capitalist system was at work in the beach resort areas. We saw places being renovated, and we figured they were privately owned businesses considering that the work appeared to be quality work.

All the cities we had visited to that point had very large apartment complexes; the Soviet system didn't allow for single-family homes. We saw a large house at the seaside and were told the original owner was hoping to get it back. When such homes were nationalized, their owners were allowed to occupy only a portion of them; other families were moved into other rooms. The young woman conducting our tour was a beautiful blonde who spoke excellent English. She was cultured; no doubt the Soviet system had placed much emphasis on education. Russian was a required language, and when those from the Baltic States visited Russia, they were supposed to speak Russian only.

In Latvia, as in Lithuania and Poland, American music was dominant. Three young boys were playing "Everybody Loves Somebody" on the street, singing in English just as if they were Americans. We remembered that in Vilnius, we had heard a woman sing in perfect English, no accent at all. When she passed our table later, I tried to speak to her and discovered she knew no English except for the lyrics of her song. We tried to learn why American music was so popular, but no one was able to tell us. But we heard everything from "Tight Fitting Jeans" to "Wake Up Little Susie" and "Cotton Balls."

Tallinn, Estonia—Tuesday, June 15, 1993

Our train was departing Riga about midnight for Tallinn. Our tickets were supposed to be furnished by Intourist, but Intourist no longer existed in the country, so we had to buy train tickets ourselves. We went to the train station in the afternoon and had an extremely difficult time finding out how to buy tickets. Finally, a gentleman with fair English was able to help us, and we bought what we thought were tickets without a sleeper compartment. We then attempted to find where we were to go to get the train; that too was difficult, but we finally succeeded, and we returned to the hotel.

The price of the tickets purchased at Latvian prices was less than $4. The price charged by our travel agent was $150. Of course, we planned to get a refund on that. We discovered that in many restaurants and other places, there were two prices—one for international and one for local—and many of the prices were based on what the market would bear. This was the practice throughout the old Soviet Union. The excessive cost of the tickets was probably not the fault of the travel agent.

We again had a hard sleeper on the train to Tallinn for a ride of about eight hours and discovered that we couldn't lock the door to our compartment. Andy unscrewed the safety catch with his knife and rigged up a safety catch that would be somewhat protective.

We were impressed with a good-looking Russian who was about twenty-three. He spoke good English and was very vocal. He was traveling with his wife; they were going from Tallinn to Helsinki by ferry. Prior to the present situation of independence, he and she couldn't have traveled to Helsinki; Finland was a capitalist country with all the goods and materials available in the Western world. It was evident the Soviets didn't want their people leaving the country and finding out how good life was on the outside.

We checked into the Hotel Viru in Tallinn; as had been our experience elsewhere, the place was comfortable. We were hungry, so we tried to buy Coke and ice cream on the street, but we didn't have the local currency. We were unable to use dollars even though the hotels, tour and rental car companies, and many other places were very anxious for dollars. We went to a department store where we thought food was available, but we were mistaken. The goods at the department store were about third quality compared to ours, but the place was very busy; maybe the goods were much more in quantity than previously. We didn't see the long lines of shoppers as we had expected we'd see. We had been told people would get in lines and wait, not knowing what was being sold. That didn't seem to be true any place we visited; goods were available even though they didn't appear to be in large quantities.

We toured Tallinn with Lira in a Mercedes; we were impressed to see new cars that had been made in Western Europe. The progress Estonia was making under the new system was most impressive.

Estonia had been founded in 1154. Tallinn, its capital, has approximately 400,000 people. It was a predominately Lutheran country; we learned there was only one Catholic church in Tallinn. We saw Catherine's Park, named after Catherine the Great of Russia. The presidential palace and amphitheater put on a big festival every five years with a choir of 20,000, a tradition that had started in 1869. In 1969, Estonians planted a hundred oak trees, the national tree of Estonia, as a tribute to the festival.

Estonia was very much like the flat Baltic States and Poland; we saw beautiful green areas, but they were somewhat unkempt, as I had mentioned earlier.

Andy and I talked to a good number of people and found them to be interesting and friendly. We met a businessman from Birmingham, England, who was in his thirties. He had opened a large carpet store in Estonia. From atop the hotel where we were eating breakfast, he pointed out the renovation in progress. He was very excited about his business. He didn't speak Estonian, but he felt he'd be without competition in the carpet business in Estonia. He was somewhat cocky; when Andy asked him if he had been to India, he answered that he was a capitalist in the carpet business in Estonia. He invited everybody to Estonia to really make money.

We boarded the MS *Tallink* ferry to go to Helsinki, Finland, about three hours away across the Gulf of Finland. American songs were as prevalent on the ferry as they were all other places we had visited. No one was able to explain the interest in American music; you'd think we were the only country in the world that produced music.

I tried to talk to one man using the few Russian words I knew. He said, "No like Rooskie. Hate Rooskie." He indicated that the Russians had sent his father to prison for ten years and his mother for fifteen years in Siberia.

Helsinki, Finland—June 16, 1993

We arrived in Helsinki at about 3:00 p.m. and took a taxi to the Vaakuna Hotel. Our travel agents had not made pickup arrangements for us there for various reasons; it was the first time we had to find a taxi ourselves. After having visited four former Soviet countries, we found Finland to be so different from them—evidence of capitalism at work. Everything was modern, and plenty of goods were readily available everywhere we looked.

Andy and I left our hotel in search of a restaurant. We were close to a commercial area and saw large department stores, restaurants— anything we wanted. We decided to eat at a Pizza Hut and get some capitalist fast food for a change, but it was closed, so we stopped at a McDonald's where I told Andy I had the best meal since leaving Atlanta. The McDonald's was loaded with customers, but the prices were perhaps close to double what we would have paid in Atlanta.

We had breakfast the next morning with a Finnish engineer who was very intelligent and enthusiastic about Finland. He mentioned that during the Finnish–Russian War in 1939–40, 500,000 men and 500,000 women served in the armed forces; Finland was a country of about 2.5 million then. I remembered seeing white-clad Finnish ski troops in Movietone newsreels at theaters back in my day; I had tremendous respect for what the Finnish did to defend themselves. Luckily, Russia evidently decided not to fight a war on the extremely cold Finnish soil, and after negotiating a truce with Russia, Finland has been completely neutral ever since, but it has depended on Russia to purchase its products. The slow Russian market had created a serious economic problem in Finland, which suffered 19 percent unemployment.

Helsinki is at about the same parallel as Anchorage, Alaska, and it gets extremely cold. However, the people there thought the previous few winters had been very mild; they thought their winters were getting warmer.

We took a bus tour around the city and saw the Temple Church, which had been built in 1860 and carved out of the center of a gigantic rock. On Friday, we bought our train tickets and visited a market in a square. We saw a great variety of vegetables, many of which had been grown in Finland. It was difficult for us to believe that vegetables could be available in mid-June in a country as cold as Finland.

We had lunch in the square; we ate a large silka fish, which would have been great if it had been warm. It was good as it was, however, and we enjoyed it and we bought fruit and beautiful sweet cherries from Bulgaria.

We took a ferry to Suomenlinna, an old fort that dated to the seventeenth century, and we took a subway to the outskirts of the city. While Helsinki had a population of about a half million in the four boroughs that make up the city, evidently, the population is much larger. The subway system was only one route running about fifteen minutes east and west.

Andy and I had developed appetites, so we found a restaurant. Andy ordered chicken with rice and gravy. I decided I wanted to go back to McDonald's for a second night. I ordered a McFeast, a vanilla shake, and french fries. The price was about $7 in Finnish marks.

A man in his early twenties heard Andy speaking English and addressed him. He was from Lithonia and was in a missionary capacity in Finland for the Church of Latter Day Saints. He had been in Finland for about nine months. According to him, only 3 percent of the Finnish population attended church. It looked as though he had his job cut out for him. We were impressed with his enthusiasm.

We got up the next morning at four so we could make our 6:26 train to St. Petersburg, about three hours away. We were excited about making our first foray into Russia. Our Finnish train was extremely clean, and it offered breakfast in a dining room. Even the toilets were extremely clean; they were a great, especially compared to the ex-Soviet trains we had been on in Lithuania and Latvia.

The flat Finnish countryside was under cultivation in every direction; we saw beautiful, impressive areas of growth. Finnish people were obviously highly motivated to do things for themselves; this was in severe contrast to the Baltic countries, where agriculture seemed to be stymied by lack of fertilizers or care. But in the ex-Communist countries, people could grow gardens only for themselves; they couldn't grow to sell as we do in America.

When we crossed into Russia, we immediately noticed a distinct lack of land under cultivation. We saw many folks working in what seemed to be their own gardens. The degree of growth and the beautiful green areas in Finland were in such contrast to those we saw in Russia. Again, perhaps it was a motivational problem.

After we crossed into Russia, we learned the dining car for breakfast would be closed for various reasons. Our Finnish locomotive was being swapped out for a Russian locomotive with a large red star on the front. Russian railroads were of a different gauge than in other parts of Europe so that trains from other countries couldn't enter Russia. This was a defensive measure—invaders would never be able to use Russian tracks. Though the Finnish and Russian tracks were of the same gauge, we were told that the Finnish locomotive couldn't operate under the Russian electrical system, so Finnish railroads didn't have ready access to Russian railroads.

We met an engineer from Charleston who was going north for sea kayaking. A blond woman thought we were all together, so she wanted to take a picture of the three of us. She spoke reasonably good English; she told me she was going a short distance into Russia to visit her father's grave. He had been killed in the war between Finland and Russia in

1939–40. She indicated to me that she didn't like "Rooskies," She had a very grim smile and was almost tearful when thinking about her dad. She and her family had lived across the border in Russia at that time but had moved back to Finland later. Evidently, her dad had joined the Finnish army even though they lived in Russia.

The first Russian city we visited when we left the train was Viborg; it was representative of other cities we had seen in the old Soviet Union—very old, dirty, and in disrepair. All the streets and sidewalks in almost every place we had visited had been clean, but there, all the buildings and the so-called infrastructure were in dire need of repair.

St. Petersburg, Russia—
Saturday, June 19, 1993

We arrived at the train station in St. Petersburg on Saturday about 1:00 p.m. and were met by a Russian with a small sign that read "Anderson and Dews." He took us to a car and driver ready to take us into town. I wasn't sure what a Russian taxi driver was supposed to look like, but this guy matched anything I could have imagined. We couldn't believe what we were seeing in the streets. He had to dodge potholes from side to side and actually at times from the left side of the street at a 45-degree angle to get back. He drove like a maniac. We couldn't believe the city that had been described as such a beautiful city was in such condition; I thought that perhaps almost nothing had been done to keep things up during the past seventy years.

We arrived at the Hotel Pribaltiyskaya; our room was satisfactory but high priced—$920 for five days, $184 a day. I asked someone later about the price he would have paid for a room at our hotel and learned it would have been about $5. I couldn't believe the disparity even though I knew there were always two prices, one for international and one for local. This is certainly understandable based on the amount of money it's said they're making.

We took a stroll to the Neva River that empties into the Gulf of Finland and back to the hotel. We met an old gentleman who must have had two pounds of coins in his pocket. He showed every one of them to us; they dated back to the early 1800s. He didn't speak English, but he never stopped talking. I would have liked to have found out about his past and ask him questions that would satisfy my inquisitive mind about the Soviet Union, especially during World War II.

The next day, we took a taxi from our somewhat remote hotel to the Hotel Astoria in the downtown area, where we could book a tour. The fare was in American dollars—$7. Susanna, our tour guide on the bus, spoke excellent English. We saw the Hermitage and the Winter Palace of Peter the Great, which had been built in the early 1700s. St. Petersburg had been founded in 1703 and was a very young city relative to other European cities.

Its name of course was changed to Leningrad after the Russian Revolution; at one time, it was called Petrograd. The Russian parliament gave permission for a referendum a couple of years earlier, and the citizens chose to rename it St. Petersburg. I asked someone about this, and he said there was no way it should have been named after Lenin since it was so closely linked to the history of Peter the Great.

The palace with all its beautiful goldwork was fantastic; it must have taken hundreds of man-years to create.

It was amazing that the Hermitage, which consists of a vast complex of buildings as well as the Winter Palace, had not been completely destroyed by the Nazis during World War II. St. Petersburg was besieged for nine hundred days, but the Nazis were turned back from the city without too much damage to the Hermitage. The shelling was supposed to have been indiscriminate; we were told that two shells fell in a particular place without destroying too much of the palace. Much of the artwork had been removed to Siberia for protection. The Nazis were turned back from the city when the Russians seized the offensive; the city was never entered.

The buildings of the Hermitage, as was the case with all the other buildings in St. Petersburg, showed little upkeep. Though the streets weren't in good shape, they were kept clean by women with brooms.

The buses continually dodged potholes. We saw many streetcars and were surprised that the tracks hadn't collapsed due to the potholes.

It was a very good day. Susanna took us to a shop where vodka was forced upon Andy and me. I gulped down my serving, about two ounces, but I couldn't handle a second serving. I forced that on Andy, who wasn't a drinker. It was very difficult to refuse Russian vodka.

We returned to the Astoria Hotel. Andy and I ate boiled chicken for 2,400 rubles, just over $2. It was beautiful to hear the theme song from *Doctor Zhivago*, or "Somewhere My Love" played on a piano in Russia. Though Boris Pasternak had been designated a "nonperson" after he wrote *Doctor Zhivago* and had it smuggled out of the Soviet Union for publication, he won a Nobel Prize for this book, I recall. When I think of the movie version, the scene that always comes to my mind is the Trans-Siberian train traveling through the Ural Mountains. It was exciting to know that within a week from that day we would be traveling through the Urals headed for Vladivostok.

The next day, Andy and I took Bus No. 7 to the downtown area since we were having a day on our own. Bus tickets were approximately 7¢ each, but we failed to pay since the bus driver was protected by glass between himself and the passengers. Knowing that almost no one would speak English, I asked the most prominent-looking person on the bus in the few Russian words I knew if she spoke English. She responded in beautiful English and told us where to get off the bus to get back to the Astoria Hotel. We asked her about paying, and she gave us a ticket, canceling it herself in a machine on the bus. We offered to pay, but she wouldn't accept payment, indicating that we could buy ten tickets for about 70¢.

Andy and I found our way to Nevsky Prospekt, the Champs de Elysee of St. Petersburg, after eating at the Astoria. We had difficulty finding what was supposed to be a mall. There was almost no identification on the front of stores, and we walked in and out, in and out, until we finally discovered the mall, a long corridor with people shoulder to shoulder and small shops on each side.

It appeared to be very inefficient; every place was staffed by at least one person, usually a cashier sitting doing almost nothing. This was labor unwisely used; it was probably an example of the Communist system in which everyone worked and profits didn't matter.

We had gone into an appliance shop the previous day with our tour guide. Andy was trying to replace his hair dryer, which had been ruined by the different electricity there. The place was run by a capitalist. Our tour guide, who was outspoken about the freedom of people, pointed out that the store ran on a profit system and was an efficient operation. It looked as though the people were gaining access to most of the products they wanted but didn't have the money to buy.

Susanna told us teachers in public schools made about $4 a day, $60 a month, whereas teachers at private schools made about $8 a day. The daily pay and the monthly total didn't seem to tally, but we nonetheless took it as an indication that their earnings were very low. The costs for most goods were very low, but Russians considered them to be very high, even at just 7¢ for a bus ride.

The next day, we toured Petrodvorets, which had been founded by Peter the Great as a summer palace. The entire city had been destroyed by the Nazis during World War II, but everything was being restored. Much of the artwork and furnishings had been taken to safety in Siberia and returned after the war. The Germans took some of the items, but they were later returned. Nonetheless, many things had been lost, so it was a huge restoration project. This was one of the few examples of the Soviet government's attempts at renovation. Considering the cost of this and all the labor involved, we wondered if we would have restored the area or used the resources for something not quite so historical.

We saw more housing units and large apartment buildings than we had seen before. Although they were prevalent all over the former Soviet territory we had visited, we were told that there were three hundred thousand units stretching for quite a few miles.

In no places other than in the country had we seen individual homes; we saw only always amazingly large complexes where thousands of people lived. From our hotel, we could see such massive residential complexes but no cars outside or evidence of people except some lights at night. The large complexes reminded me of Pruitt-Igoe in St. Louis, a large complex under the federal housing program that became the worst example in the country of people living in such large complexes. Windows were always broken, things were torn to pieces, items were thrown out windows—even refrigerators—and the US government decided that type of housing complex didn't work.

Yana, one of our tour guides, was pursuing a degree in English at the University of Leningrad; she had two years to go. She said they called the university the Catacombs because almost nothing had been done to the place since the day of the czars. She was very interesting; I sat beside her on the bus on the return trip, asking many questions about life there and touching a few times on things that could have been somewhat embarrassing. She has been only to Helsinki. I asked her about her impression of this very successful country with the fantastic economy that reminded us of any great city in the United States. She wasn't favorably impressed. I asked her about all the goods available, but that hadn't impressed her either. I wondered if she just didn't understand what life was like outside Russia or if she was simply dedicated to the old system and just hadn't had the opportunity to smell the roses.

I asked Yana about a sign in front of our hotel that indicated an Italian restaurant was close by. She said, "Oh yes, the Venice is very close." She said she lived very close to it. I invited her to dinner; she gave me her telephone number. I was to call her about six that evening.

We got back to the hotel somewhat late, about a quarter to seven. I had read that Russians expect extreme punctuality. I called her, and she said, "It is now impossible since you are almost an hour late." We had a nice conversation. I wished her the best, and she did the same for my family and me. She indicated that the Venice was very expensive but was her favorite restaurant. She had seemed anxious to go. I regretted very much that we were unable to take her to dinner and talk to a Russian about the things I was interested in.

We did go to the Venice, which was in walking distance of the hotel. The menu was in Russian, so Andy and I were unable to order until a waitress with very limited English explained the menu. Andy's lasagna cost 500 rubles, about 45¢; my spaghetti was less than that. When Andy ordered a Coke, the waitress pointed out that it was $2, which she considered unusually expensive. So did we. We ordered hot tea.

Incidentally, the spaghetti and lasagna were good; I ordered a second serving of the spaghetti. It was certainly one of the better meals we had in the old Soviet Union areas. The total meal, including service charge, came to about 4,200 rubles—less than $4. This was the restaurant that Yana had warned us was very expensive.

During our meal, we saw four young people wearing Duke University shirts. They were as happy to see us as we were to see them, and we had a great conversation. They had been there about five weeks; they had come to study Russian and were leaving in two weeks. One of them, Lily Bradford, lived in Atlanta, in Sandy Springs; I asked her to call Marie when she got back to Atlanta. She said they ordered pizza, which was less than $1.

The next day, we went to Pushkin and Pavlovsk, about twenty-five miles from St. Petersburg. The route we took was interesting. We stopped at a supermarket that was fourth class by American standards. We saw about six checkout lanes with registers such as those we used thirty or forty years ago. Andy stood in a line of about ten people to buy some candy at the candy counter, which had two cashiers. We wondered, since the candy was prepackaged, why we couldn't pay for it in the regular checkout lanes. We saw a line of about a dozen people buying meat. We assumed that their purchases had been weighed and marked so they could pay there.

On the previous day on Nevsky Prospekt, we saw butchers in a very small shop where meat was hanging. They were chopping the meat with the largest cleavers I'd ever seen. I thought they must have gotten very tired at the end of the day chopping through those big bones. I wondered why they didn't use saws. The meat was very crudely cut, and customers had to go to a cashier to pay for it, get a receipt, then go back and get their meat. This required roughly two people to handle the transaction three times. The Russians had had productivity problems for so many years and were probably trying to keep everyone working in a workers' society. While the rate of unemployment was high when we were there, back before perestroika, it was low.

We passed an impressive monument dedicated to the lifting of the siege of Leningrad after the nine hundred days the Nazis had tried to conquer the city. It was a magnificent monument dedicated to the soldiers and all the people who had saved Leningrad from destruction. It was a big round circle of granite or marble with many sculpted figures. The open end of the monument symbolized the opening of Leningrad after the siege.

We saw some very low hills in the countryside that were about the highest we had seen so far, all the countries being fairly level. Very few things were growing. We saw a collective farm, but the amount of growth wasn't impressive. Our tour guide, Natasha, said that it was too cold there to grow very much. We tactfully pointed out later the agriculture we had seen in Finland, which was farther north. We assumed these people had been dictated to on what they should say and do; the fact that everything had been owned by the government in the past gave people little motivation to work hard and make things grow.

Collective farms in Russia had never been very productive. In fact, the country had to buy wheat by the hundreds of millions of tons from the United States and Canada as well as other foodstuffs. The old Russian workers' axiom that "They pretend to pay us and we pretend to work" seemed to apply under the collective farm method. Someone once said, "Democracy is the worst possible system, except for all the rest." The collective farm system had failed not only in producing crops but also distributing them; much of what was grown rotted before it could be shipped where it was needed due to the lack of a good distribution system.

Natasha was interesting and spoke very good English. She was, of course, accompanied by her driver, Boris, who drove like a Russian taxi driver. We liked him; he was fairly funny even though he didn't speak English. I told him with a smile that his moustache looked like Stalin's, meaning it was very nice; I didn't want to offend him. I'm not sure he understood, but I think so. We saw the only statue of Lenin that we had seen in St. Petersburg. It was impressive; we wondered why it hadn't been pulled down along with many others.

Andy asked Natasha about all the potholes; Natasha passed the comment along to Boris. Boris said something that included, "New York," and Natasha said that Boris had said we had potholes in New York.

Leaving Pushkin, the town named for one of Russia's favorite poets, we went to the nearby city of Pavlovsk. This was another attractive, small town with another palace that had been occupied by a disliked son of Catherine. Since she couldn't stand to have him living with her, she built him that very sumptuous palace. No wonder the people disliked the czars—all their palaces and splendor came at the people's cost.

We returned to the hotel and paid $56 for four and a half hours (which was cut to four for charge purposes) for the car, the driver, and the tour guide who spoke English—a very good price.

We had two pizzas and two cups of tea at the Venice for about 4,200 rubles, less than $4. It was only fair, but it was Pizza Hut–thin, which we liked.

We went downtown to use a low-cost telephone the Duke University group had told us about near the Hermitage and Nevsky Prospekt. The business center in the Hotel Pribaltiyskaya wanted $14 per minute for telephone calls or faxes. Using our room phone, through ATT, would have cost $5 for the first minute, and the hotel would have added $5 for each minute after that. We thought that was too expensive.

Bus No. 7, having evidently stopped for the day, passed us up, and another bus didn't come along in the next thirty minutes. A young man, speaking fair English, decided that he would cancel his bus trip and walked us about a half mile to the underground metro. He boarded with us and paid for us evidently. He showed us where to get off the train, very close to the telephone building where we could make low-cost calls. This was typical Russian treatment; whenever we sought help, people were outstanding in their willingness to help us.

We had difficulty making a call. With help from at least three or four people, we finally learned we had to get a number from a cashier and go to certain phones to make calls to the States. After our conversations, we reported to the cashier, who issued a printout for the time charged. My call was $8.15, and I know it was over fifteen minutes long. Andy and I called again the next day, and we talked for thirteen minutes for 6,864 rubles—$6.30. What a deal compared to any other type of call we could have made!

Andy and found a Russian cafe and saw lines of people stretching for more than a block. We found that new entrepreneurs were selling goods on the street. It was a very crowded situation. We entered the café and stood in line for about ten minutes with about eight people in front of us. We couldn't believe it was so slow. Andy ordered a hamburger, and I ordered something that looked like rice. Andy says he cannot smell things, and I have doubts after seeing him eat food on our trip up to that point that he can taste either. It certainly had to be a pleasure for his wife to cook for him.

Back on the street, Andy ordered something like an ice cream sandwich, and I followed suit. I ate a pack of peanut butter crackers I had brought from home, thinking I could locate a Coca-Cola, but I was unable to do that until I got back to the hotel.

We were leaving St. Petersburg in about two and a half hours for Moscow with a very good feeling for the Russian people. They were so kind and friendly in situations far too numerous to remember or mention. We believed they really liked Americans. I wondered if they felt about us the way we felt about them five or six years earlier, before Gorbachev and *perestroika* and *glasnost*—reconstruction and openness. I recalled Margaret Thatcher saying about Mikhail Gorbachev when he first visited Britain, "I can do business with this man." At the time, I thought she must have been dreaming, but most people today would give Gorbachev credit for creating a very different kind of Russia with an unintentional result of a breakup of the Soviet Union and its associated fifteen states. Considering the very poor state of the infrastructure we saw everywhere there, I think Gorbachev must have seen the handwriting on the wall and decided they had no choice other than to become a democratic and capitalist society.

Everyone in St. Petersburg loves the city, which is called the Venice of the North. It has canals leading to the Neva River. While it's unlike Venice in architecture, its many waterways and bridges resemble those in Venice. Andy commented about the city looking much better on our fifth day than it had when we arrived. We think we had become accustomed to it, and I think that's the reason Russians didn't see the decay of their buildings, roads, and parks in St. Petersburg.

St. Petersburg, a city of over five million, had been founded in the early 1700s. It was renamed for V. I. Lenin, the founder of communism in Russia. Karl Marx and Friedrich Engels, I believe both Germans, were the real founders (for the lack of a better word) of communism or Marxism, as I guess it was called. Lenin was perhaps the first person to create communism in a large country. Moscow became the capital in 1924 after his death.

We left St. Petersburg with a good feeling about its culture and art, but the sidewalks were paved with asphalt, and we saw a lot of water puddled in areas where there was dirt. But the sidewalks and the streets were kept clean by middle-aged or elderly women who continually swept them.

One morning, when we were on a tour bus, we saw a woman sweeping streetcar tracks in front of a stopped streetcar. The street was almost demolished under the tracks; Andy wished for his camera to take a photo of a scene that depicted real life in the old Soviet Union. However, in many cases, our most vivid and memorable scenes were those we were unable to record.

At the airport in St. Petersburg, a Russian in a uniform asked us if we were Americans. He was about sixty, but he looked younger; he worked for Aeroflot. He had lived in Africa, in Mali, for about three years, had lived in France and Germany as well, and spoke four languages, including English, better than most of us. I asked him his name; he told me, "Yuri Gagarin." He was the Russian cosmonaut who was the first to orbit the earth. I think he was pleased we remembered that. When he asked us the name of the first person to set foot on the moon, neither one of us could remember it just then. Yuri said it was Neil Armstrong.

It seemed that everyone we ran into knew much about America, its people, and its history. We got the impression that they liked Americans; we never felt threatened or disliked by anyone we met there.

Moscow—Thursday Night, June 24, 1993

Our first flight in Russia was aboard an Aeroflot plane much like an American 727. The luggage compartments were open, and the seats were very thin, not plush at all. However, it was just a one-hour flight. We weren't served anything until we were ready to land, and then it was only about one-third of a Spritelike liquid.

We couldn't believe what we saw in the dark, gray, dirty building where we had to retrieve our luggage. This airport for a city of nine million was unbelievably dirty, and its sidewalks and everything else were in very poor shape. We discovered later that we had arrived at a domestic terminal; a new, big terminal was reserved for international flights. We had to walk perhaps two hundred yards from the plane to the terminal. A truck with a low-cost trailer attached to it served as a bus and picked up as many passengers as it could hold and, we believed, took them to another terminal.

We retrieved our luggage, and our transfer people met us to take us to the hotel. They were very prompt, as had been the others who had met us during our trip. We headed into town. Everything was very unattractive; we saw nothing that was aesthetically pleasing. Andy saw a large building and decided it was the main terminal. We were at Sheremetyevo Airport. I had some doubts about that, but we discovered the next morning in some literature that it was the main airport and would probably do credit to a city of Moscow's size. In any case, it appeared that gondolas or walkways out to planes were perhaps not used in the country. We walked on mobile stairways to get to the terminal.

On the way into the city, things looked much better. It looked much like areas of almost any other city. We saw some beautiful, large complexes that would have been considered public housing in the States, but again, we saw no single homes.

Moscow had attempted to keep its population down to nine million by not building new apartments or by perhaps not approving people moving to the city except to replace those who died. Although criticized by many as being very dirty, Moscow seemed more modern than St. Petersburg. We saw much construction going on and figured it was due to foreign investment.

Coca-Cola had been in Russia for the previous two or three years, while Pepsi had been there for perhaps ten years. A word to the wise here—Pepsi had better get on the ball. Coca-Cola had done a promotional campaign throughout the old Soviet Union and Finland that was unbelievable. Every place we went, we saw the world's most recognized trademark even though it was very expensive. Andy paid $2 for one at lunch, but most of the time on the street, they were $1. I had drunk more Cokes in the past two and a half weeks than I had in the past two years. Coke seemed well ahead of Pepsi at that time.

We checked into room 1419 at the Intourist Hotel and were very disappointed with how small it was. At $763 for four nights, it was the most expensive room I'd ever stayed in, and it had the least value. We had difficulty finding a place to set our baggage. Two twin beds were side by side; I felt Andy and I would end up sleeping together. Andy shoved the beds apart. I didn't know if he didn't want to be that close to me because of my snoring. We had accused each other of snoring on the first night of our trip. I told him that if he snored the next night, I'd kiss him. I figured he'd stay awake all night fearing that and I would be able to sleep. We settled in and headed downstairs to eat, as we hadn't eaten much or well that day.

We discovered in a "dollar" restaurant, one that accepted dollars, that prices were very high. A simple plate of spaghetti was over $15.

We decided we wouldn't pay such prices; we headed back to our room and ate peanut butter crackers and three Oreos each. We toasted each other with two glasses of water.

In the five countries we had visited, including Russia, the hotel bathrooms were equipped with hand-held showers. In a couple of cases, they could be hung on the wall, and we were able to take fairly decent showers. But the shower curtains were missing or were too short to keep water off the floor. In the Intourist, we had no curtains, the shower couldn't be hung on the wall, and I found myself stooping in the bathtub to get myself wet, standing up to soap myself, and stooping again to get the soap off. While it was inconvenient, we soon became accustomed to it, and it wasn't a real problem.

We had known that we would face many situations we hadn't been exposed to in the past. One was food. However, we were very adaptable. Andy came to realize I just didn't like the taste of the food though it looked like our food in the United States. Nonetheless, we were able to get along okay with the food without becoming too disagreeable.

Breakfast was usually different lunchmeats, cheese, and vegetables, including cucumbers and tomatoes. Most of the bread was sliced and was the same in every place we had visited. We had rolls on occasion, but we learned there wasn't a hot piece of bread in all Europe. I'd not been drinking coffee until I had instant coffee at the Intourist. Each morning, I drank coffee first, as I did at home, and then picked at the food enough to get by for the rest of the day. Almost every day, we ate hard-boiled eggs, which were available everywhere. Some of the food was perhaps porridge, something I didn't recognize.

We took a tour of the Kremlin our first morning in Moscow, which was no more than two blocks from the Intourist and visible from there. We were excited. Tamara, our tour guide, spoke very good English and was very entertaining. She told us about the Kremlin, its origin, and the history of the buildings, including churches, inside the Kremlin. It was evident that most of the churches weren't in use, but at least they hadn't been torn down in this atheistic and Communist society. We saw the largest cannon in the world in the Kremlin and perhaps the largest bell in the world. It had been built several hundred years ago, and at two hundred tons, it was too big to lift. When it was placed on a wooden framework for storage, the framework burned, the bell dropped, and a large hole was broken in it. Both the fragment and the bell were in view.

The grounds of the Kremlin were the most manicured of any place we had been up to that point. We saw Stalin's apartment in what I believe was called the palace. He was the last head of the old Soviet Union to live at the Kremlin. We invited Tamara to lunch, and we had some very good conversation with her. Her son, who was about thirty, was a university professor. His specialty was forensic medicine— criminal science. Like almost everyone with whom we talked, she was very disappointed with the rate of inflation and the pay in Russia. Her son made 40,000 rubles a month, but that was only about $38. She said that since he was a bachelor, he had to pay about 5,000 rubles as a bachelor's income tax.

Tamara told us that riding the metro, the underground, cost six rubles—less than a penny, but to Russians, it was expensive. It was only a short time earlier that it had cost only a few kopeks. I had trouble remembering whether there were ten or a one hundred kopeks in a ruble. I wondered how many years it would take for that society before its people would make public transportation self-supporting.

Tamara said that a teacher in an elementary school made $25 a month. That income was certainly relative in a country such as Russia, but we did get a sense of how costly things were for Russians, as opposed to us, who were paying so few dollars for so many things priced in rubles.

After finishing lunch and our tour, Andy and I were anxious to get to Red Square. We were about two blocks away from it, and I discovered Red Square wasn't quite as large as I thought it would be. The Kremlin and Lenin's tomb were on one side, St. Basil's Cathedral was at one end, and another church, a museum, was at another end. The GUM department store, one of the world's largest, was across the street.

I was impressed with Lenin's mausoleum, which has "Lenin" in Russian on the front. It was beautiful; it had been constructed in very good taste, and it blended well with its surroundings. I had an interest in the modern Soviet Union, its peoples' thinking and politics—what made them tick. As I gazed at Lenin's tomb, I could almost hear the rumblings of large missiles and other military equipment going by in November each year in commemoration of the October 1917 revolution, I believe. The parades were always awesome; Stalin and other heads of government stood atop Lenin's tomb to view the parade. I always thought they were flexing their muscles for all the world to see, and I certainly was one of those who feared what they might do to us. I believed I could recall most of the heads of the Soviet state back from Stalin's days, so I found the place very interesting.

We headed to the GUM department store, which was nice compared to other retail establishments we'd visited in the old Soviet Union. It was two stories tall, and it had three large shopping areas; it was in effect a mall. It was crowded, and Andy took videos while I took photos.

Shops, many of which were probably privatized and operated by international companies, occupied the store along with what were still many state-run operations. These small shops offered merchandise that couldn't have been purchased a few years earlier, but the shops weren't as impressive as American department stores or those in other Western countries such as Finland.

We saw a bar at one end. I told Andy I'd buy him a drink. The closest thing I could find to something I thought he would drink was Amaretto. It was a large amount for $3. I bought a glass of beer for, I believe, $2. The bar took rubles and dollars. Recognizing us as Westerners or even perhaps as Americans, the young, good-looking bartender refused Andy's rubles. He wanted to bring in many more times what a Russian would pay.

An American schoolteacher came up; we discovered she spoke Russian well. She had been speaking Russian for ten years and taught Russian in a California school. She was very aloof; she didn't want to converse with us, and she rebuffed my efforts to converse with her and learn more about things and people. I believe Andy asked her whether she paid rubles; she said yes but didn't say how many. She was recognized, I suppose, as being Russianized or on a special mission and was charged only rubles, probably because she spoke Russian so well.

We left the bar. Andy's curiosity got us into the department store itself. I saw an Estee Lauder shop; my daughter Jane worked at one in Tallahassee. I was excited about that enough to take a photograph so she could see her company's store in Russia. I understood from a *60 Minutes* program that Estee Lauder was probably out of business and had paid fantastic sums of money because of some bureaucratic problem in the Soviet Union. However, they were still in business there.

Because of my fondness for the Estee Lauder salespeople I had met through Jane, I wanted to take pictures with two very attractive girls. They permitted that with smiles, and I was sure Marie was going to be very disappointed when she saw I was somehow able to smile in those pictures.

We returned to the hotel, and I coerced Andy into going to the No. 2 McDonald's that had recently opened nearby. We learned that the McDonald's accepted only rubles, which we were almost out of. No agency was open for exchange. We went to the street, where some entrepreneurs were exchanging rubles. Some refused to exchange our dollars for rubles, but we found one who was willing to give us 900 rubles for $1 when it should have been about 1,060 rubles. I decided it was worth about $1.20 to eat that evening, so we headed to McDonald's.

My Big Mac, shake, and fries cost slightly more than 2,800 rubles, under $3. That made me wonder if McDonald's was making any money in Russia; however, the prices there were based on what Muscovites could afford. The fries tasted like the grease had been used too long, and I didn't really like my Big Mac, though I had enjoyed almost the same meal in Helsinki. I felt that at least the vanilla shake was a profitable item. Andy was able to sacrifice his taste and endure a McDonald's hamburger with fries and a Coke.

The next day, Saturday, June 26, we decided to view Lenin's body inside his mausoleum. We took our umbrellas because it was a windy, wet day, but out desire to see Lenin overcame the horrible weather. We walked right in and circled Lenin in his glass coffin. My impression was that he was better looking than most of his pictures showed; he looked as though he were sleeping. He had a very strong face, but his hands seemed smaller than average. It was most impressive; it was evident that in the past, the Communists revered the founder of the Soviet Union.

We went to grave sites behind his tomb, and I looked for names in Russian that I might recognize. My study of the Russian alphabet before making this trip helped me recognize the names. The first I saw was Chernenko, the sixth head of state upon his appointment several years earlier; I believe he was succeeded by Mikhail Gorbachev. The next was Andropov, the head of state just prior to Chernenko and former head of the KGB. Both of these men were unhealthy and had lived for a very short time after their appointments; they had perhaps been appointed as a tribute to their past contributions to the Communist Party. I might have them reversed as far as their time of serving.

I knew that Khrushchev, who banged on a table at the United Nations with his shoe in the early days after Stalin's death and uttered the phrase, "We will bury you," had become a "nonperson" in the Soviet Union and that the Russians had been very embarrassed at his antics. Maybe that was the reason he had been replaced as the head of state while he was on vacation on the Black Sea and the reason he hadn't been buried with the other heads of state behind Lenin's mausoleum.

When the coup occurred in the summer about two years ago against Gorbachev, I wondered in jest why he hadn't learned not to take Black Sea vacations when his country was undergoing strife.

By evening, I was very hungry for something tasty and typically American. I remembered a Pizza Hut a few blocks from the hotel on Tverskaya Street, formerly Gorky Street. Andy was agreeable, so off we went for some good, old Americana. We ordered a medium pizza, Andy had a Pepsi (since Pizza Hut was owned by Pepsi), and I ordered a beer. The total was $22, much more expensive than in America.

We left Pizza Hut and were walking toward the largest McDonald's in the world and encountered a police-vs.-public situation. We didn't know what was going on; crowds of people were raising Cain with a policeman on our side of what appeared to be a large Russian jeep. We couldn't understand what was happening, but it was very serious, and somewhat surprisingly, the policeman was taking so long to put down the unrest or whatever the problem was. Andy and I, standing on the sidewalk, encountered two women who were a part of the resistance, and they proved to be very interesting. One was perhaps explaining the situation to me, and I said, "Roosky is mad," making sure that a smile accompanied that statement. They laughed, and Andy and I laughed with them. We let them know we liked the Rooskies and we thought they liked us too.

Andy noticed one of the women pull out of her bag a large sausage, about three inches in diameter and fifteen inches long. She shook it as though she was going to hit someone over the head with it, and we laughed. When she returned it to the bag, we saw a plucked chicken with its head and feet still intact in her bag. We laughed at that as well; we were where plucked chickens were taken from the markets unwrapped.

We spent some time with the women and had fun. I mentioned in two Russian words I happened to know that one was pretty and one was beautiful. They understood my bad Russian and seemed to like it, as all women like to be called beautiful.

We headed to McDonald's and felt that, including standing room, the place could have held 2,000. Andy and I ordered chocolate sundaes and paid about 80¢ each for those, which could be very profitable in Russia.

That ended the day. I thought about calling Marie even though I had talked with her a couple of days earlier. The price would be right, $6 or $8 for ten or fifteen minutes or more. We figured that it would be difficult to call once we were on the Trans-Siberian. I could never determine if I was in the right line for a phone; I encountered Pakistanis or Middle Easterners with no knowledge of English. I finally discovered I was in the right line. I received a security number to use and a telephone booth, and I dialed Marie. Our answering machine came on. I had to dial a three to activate the timing of the call, but that reversed our answering machine and started the recording again. I gave up. I decided to try her sometime Monday morning even though it would awaken her sometime after midnight.

I tried again at five thirty Monday morning but received no answer. I tried later in the day and got Marie about 2:00 a.m. I felt better having done that as we were anticipating a 5,800-mile train ride to Vladivostok, not counting the five-day trip to Mongolia.

The next day, Sunday, we had a free day to do anything we desired. We decided to go back to the Kremlin. One of the sights Andy wanted to see was the Tomb of the Unknown Soldier. It was simple yet impressive, and we took pictures. A "flame of glory" burned eternally. Inscribed on the foundation of the tomb was, "Your name is unknown, but your deed is eternal." This was as touching as the rituals at the Tomb of the Unknown Solider in Arlington National Cemetery. The Russians care about their families as much as we do about ours.

Adjacent to the tomb were several granite blocks inscribed in Russian with cities such as Leningrad, Moscow, Stalingrad, and others I could recognize. These were very big battles; and thinking about those battles that I remember during World War II, I was glad we hadn't had to fight the Russians, especially on their own soil.

The Kremlin grounds were immaculately kept; we saw more flowers there than we had anywhere else on the trip. We wondered why flowers were so prolific in Finland, for example, but almost nonexistent in Russia. My guess was that the 280 million people who occupied the former Soviet Union had learned over the years not to care too much about the way things were.

We met four women from Salt Lake City; we took a couple of pictures and had great conversation with them. They were traveling from Moscow to Berlin by train. They were fun and very interesting. A few minutes later, we ran into them again, and they wanted to take pictures of us. In my opinion, they had fallen in love with Andy, not me.

We also visited the armory and saw Russian small arms, rifles, pistols, and horse-drawn carriages that were huge beyond belief. They were beautiful; Andy and I had never seen anything like them.

Tamara, our guide on the Kremlin grounds a few days earlier, had suggested that we obtain tickets to see the *Nutcracker*. We arrived at an old, dilapidated building that looked very big, like the Parthenon, and was named the Palace of Congresses. Unlike the outside, the inside was magnificent, abounding in marble throughout, extremely well maintained, and an example of the emphasis Russians place on the arts. The *Nutcracker* was performed beautifully in a Christmas spirit, of course, with large packages and a Christmas tree symbol on the back screen. Andy and I enjoyed it.

We then looked for a place to eat. We found a restaurant where we spent $55, including the service charge. The meal was fair, and the wine was very weak.

On returning to the hotel, we learned that our train was leaving shortly after noon the next day, eight hours earlier than we had anticipated. That was a surprise; it affected our next day's plans to ride the metro and see Gorky Park and the American embassy. We decided we could do that on our return visit to Moscow.

The Trans-Siberian Train—June 28, 1993

Andy and I had good service when we left the hotel for the train station. The train was nice, nothing luxurious, but it had a very clean toilet. We wouldn't need to put clothespins on our noses on that train.

Security on trains had been our greatest fear since our incident on the train to Latvia. We attempted to fit in a piece of wood that we'd found in Moscow to secure the door and prevent its opening from the outside. This wasn't possible, but Andy in his most persistent manner finally communicated with the conductor of our car to give him a key to the room so we could lock it when we left; that enabled us to eat together. We ate lunch, a reasonably tasty soup with bread and hot tea that, as I recall, cost us less than $1. In the evening, we had steak and eggs with tea for 1,600 rubles. Communication was extremely difficult on the train, but most Russians working with the public knew a few words of English such as *eggs* or *zoup*.

Our first large city stop was Yaroslavl. We could view only the train station, which was in need of a capitalist rejuvenation.

During the trip, we spoke with several people, including a German family that had driven the Pan American highway from Tierra del Fuego in Argentina all the way to Tallahassee, Florida, and farther to New York. They were taking the Trans-Siberian to Mongolia, and from there into the southern provinces that were republics of the old Soviet Union, all the way back home. Quite a trip!

The landscape was just about the same in that the country was very flat. I supposed the continental glacier, if that term applied to this part of the world, must have made it flat. We saw trees lining the tracks, large fields, and small villages of old-looking houses. Some of the houses were painted, and we saw people working in the gardens next to them. Boy, how I would have liked to have had some of those vegetables! They must have invented potatoes in that country; every place we saw a garden, we saw potatoes in unbelievable quantities. We hoped they could get their potatoes to the market instead of having them rot in the fields due to lack of transportation and distribution systems.

Just before 11:30 p.m., Andy and I decided we were ready for bed. We heard a faint tap on the door. We looked at each other, wondering what the tap was for and why it had been so quiet. After hesitating for a few seconds, Andy opened the door and was confronted by a Russian who had a cigarette in his hand. He asked for a light. Andy and I noticed he had a key in his hand just like the one Andy had secured from the conductor. Andy and I had the same thought. He had knocked to see if our compartment was empty. Andy asked him why he had the key. I let him know we wouldn't be easy targets. I said, "You bring you're a★★ back to this compartment tonight, you'll be in big trouble." It was evident by the expression on my face what I had meant. He said something that perhaps indicated he was somewhat tough himself. We closed the door and were very much concerned about the rest of the night, even though Andy secured the door to some extent with a broken piece of the stick.

The next morning, we told the German teacher next to us about the incident and discovered that the prospective thief had pulled the same stunt on them.

We knew that we must have been spotted pretty easily; we felt that we were considered lucrative prey for thieves that were becoming more numerous in this embryonic capitalistic society. We decided to find something to secure the door better while we were sleeping from then on.

The next day, we traveled the remainder of an approximate thousand miles from Moscow to Ekaterinburg. The scenery was much as it had been the previous day, with large, beautiful spruce trees on either side of the track for miles. We believed they had been planted to keep snow from blowing onto the tracks in the flat countryside.

We were amazed that we didn't see any animals. The area certainly couldn't be considered a wilderness area; we went through some large cities as well as many villages and farms along the way.

As we approached Ekaterinburg, someone said we were approaching the dividing line between Europe and Asia. I ran to get the camera, called to Andy, and got back to the window in time to take a picture of an obelisk about fifteen feet tall. I believe it had the inscriptions "Europe" and "Asia." It was my first trip to Asia, but Andy had spent time in Japan and the South Pacific while in the US Navy. We were then in the Urals, and even though the mountain range was well known throughout the world, from my perspective, they were only big hills, nothing that anyone from Georgia or Virginia would consider mountains.

We were somewhat concerned about someone picking us up in Ekaterinburg because our train schedule had been advanced by eight hours. However, Intourist had evidently notified them to pick us up, and within five minutes, we were in a van with Arkady, our driver. He was an enthusiastic soul, certainly among the most gregarious people we had met in our travels.

I knew only two things about Ekaterinburg since there was nothing in Fodor's manual. I knew that President Yeltsin's career had bloomed in Ekaterinburg and that the Romanovs, Czar Nicholas II and his family of five, were killed there. Our driver pointed out what appeared to be a very crude monument in an open dirt area and indicated it had something to do with Czar Nicholas II. We stopped and took pictures. It was an exciting moment. The previous year, I had read an account that the story of the murders of the Romanovs had been true. I believe genetic tests proved they were the Romanovs.

Most of us in America know about Anastasia; it appears that she was also proven to have been killed, but I'm not sure about this since there have been many stories about some claiming to be Anastasia over the years. The czar had lost power close to the end of the revolution, which started in Leningrad; his family had been moved to Ekaterinburg, and they were killed sometime after 1917.

We checked into the Hotel Oktyabrskaya and discovered that for the first time we had separate rooms. We felt more secure sleeping in the same room, but singles were okay for a change. We got there about 8:00 p.m., or so we thought. We hadn't realized we had crossed two time zones; it was actually ten, and the dining room was closed. Arkady took us to a restaurant and ate with us. He thoroughly enjoyed his meal. We ate a meat in what looked like a transparent jelly covering it about an inch thick. Arkady bit into it as if it were the tastiest morsel ever made by mortal woman. Andy and I tried it but couldn't handle it even though I worried that might embarrass Arkady.

The next morning, we discovered that the water wasn't hot. I put on my shirt, pants, and shoes—no underwear—and went downstairs to check on the hot water. The receptionist couldn't speak English, but I heard two people speaking English. They were Americans; one was from Philadelphia, but I can't remember where the other one was from. They said the hot water was furnished by the city but had been cut off for maintenance for a month.

I went up to the room. Andy had discovered the same problem. He suggested a marine bath to me. I didn't know what that meant. I suggested he take a whore's bath—you wash your eyes and armpits and use discretion with everything else. We thought that since we had been on the train all night and hadn't had a bath in two days, we should take a shower. My shower had just a trickle of cold water, and that hurt considerably more than a real deluge of water. Believe you me, Siberian water is raunchy cold when it hits the body. However, we were able to make it through the ordeal and even have a few laughs about it later. It wasn't very comforting to know we'd be staying at that hotel for three nights.

It was extremely difficult to find anyone in the Oktyabrskaya Hotel who spoke English. We found a small, private-business service center furnishing translations, interpreting, and other services needed by foreign businesspeople who were really on the move in Russia at that time. Natasha, one of the women there, spoke English reasonably well; she called around to find someone who could take us on a tour.

Ekaterinburg, Catherineburg, was named after Catherine the Great; its population is about 1.3 million. Almost nothing there would attract tourists other than perhaps the Czar Nicholas II killing site and the fact that President Yeltsin had built his career there. Since it had been a closed city with no tourists, no one had reason to develop tour services.

Our attempts to hire a car met negative results. Natasha made a call and came back with a $200 price to visit the Romanov killing site. We told her that was ridiculous, way too high a price, at least for Russia. Ena, who spoke exceptionally good English (she had lived in England for the previous three years), told us as well that $200 was ridiculous. We said we'd pay $30, and Ena thought that was reasonable.

Natasha made a call to a tourist service, or so we thought, but it was to the director of archives for the Ekaterinburg region. We were very surprised when Natasha accompanied us with a driver on the trip. We met the director, Stanislaw Menininski, and were impressed with his ebullient manner. He was enthusiastic and intelligent and had a great voice. He immediately brought out tea for us. I wish we could have understood him directly, but Natasha did a beautiful job interpreting.

Stanislaw brought out what I thought were original records from the archives. The first envelope was written in cursive ; I was able to pick out the word *Romanov*, and the date on the envelope was March 19, 1918, the date on which the orders were issued to kill the Romanovs.

Stanislaw took about three hours to deliver his message, and he took us back to the killing site, which we had seen the day before. We had seen pictures of the building in which the murders had taken place, but it had been demolished sometime in the late '80s. It was understood that Boris Yeltsin, secretary and top man in the Communist Party in the Sverdlovsk region at that time, issued the order. They couldn't quite understand that either, according to my understanding. While I had read an account of the killings and proof that the Romanovs had been found, I was thinking that one man had killed all seven in the family, as impossible as that may sound. Stanislaw pointed out that "Yarolski" shot Nicholas in the back of the head. Supposedly, a total of eleven shooters committed the killings. There were others killed at the same time as the Romanovs.

Bear in mind that the Romanovs had been brought from St. Petersburg to Ekaterinburg; someone said Czar Nicholas II asked if they were going to be killed. This was prior to the October 1917 revolution, when Lenin came to power.

We saw a signed document on which Stanislaw spent quite some time. The queen of Serbia and her husband were among those to be executed. The queen had asked that her husband be spared, and she was given permission to go to Moscow to beg for his life. While she failed to save his life, she saved her own, but forever after, she was incommunicado so secrecy could be maintained.

Stanislaw gave us a book in Russian about the killings and entered our names and a message in Russian that we couldn't decipher. Upon return from the killing site, he served coffee and vodka, which tasted very good.

We mentioned that we had visited Lenin's tomb in Moscow, and I told him about viewing the October celebrations, which I believe occurred the first part of November with the massive military. I told him I was very glad that Americans and Russians were friends and didn't have to battle each other. He said that it had been a sad period in their history and that everything done by the Soviets was for the military, not the people. That, as I have mentioned before, was evident throughout Poland, the one Soviet-bloc country we had visited; the Baltic countries, which were never recognized by the United States as being a part of the Soviet Union; and Russia itself.

Since communication is always difficult even with fellow Americans, you can imagine the difficulty we had not speaking the language. We discovered that Natasha was charging us for her services, which was understandable even though we hadn't known that in the beginning. We paid her $12 an hour for three hours plus $5 for something else. Andy and I both paid her since she had been extremely nice and was beautiful. After having been gone for about twenty-five days, we fell madly in love with her. However, we couldn't do anything about it partially because of the age disparity and the fact that Andy and I were married with wonderful wives to whom we didn't want to confess any such thing upon our return.

The second day was completely free, but we had great difficulty hiring a driver to see the city even though we had seen much of it already. We spoke to someone who knew English at Intourist who promised to call us back within an hour but didn't. The business center made a call for us, and Intourist said they'd be there with a car and driver in ten minutes, but that took about thirty minutes.

We saw the city at a cost of $15 an hour for Ena, the interpreter (but not the Ena at the business center), and our tour was enjoyable. We got back to our hotel and invited Arkady to have dinner with us at a Chinese restaurant, the only Chinese restaurant we had seen on our trip. We didn't see any Mexican or other ethnic restaurants anyplace we visited except for the Italian restaurant in St. Petersburg.

The Chinese restaurant was a new, entrepreneurial operation run by Caucasians. The food bore no resemblance whatsoever to the Chinese food we were used to in the States; I didn't enjoy it, but it was edible. Arkady ate with great delight. The total meal was approximately $13, which we paid for in rubles.

Arkady took us on more visits around the city on the way back to the hotel, and we stopped at a large lake where children were swimming with a collie, which was also having a great time.

Ena told us how much she made working for Intourist. We talked about conditions in the country; she was very outspoken about the new system and didn't like it, as was the case with many other people we talked to. They were having a very hard time providing for themselves. Inflation was severe, and she told us that she'd never, for instance, be able to own a car on the 15,000 rubles ($15) she earned monthly. And she was fluent in German, knew some English, and worked for Intourist, which was a governmental agency. She told us that a new Lada, a very basic Russian car, would cost about eight million rubles. I figured it would take her more than forty-four years to pay for one. The lowest class of automobile we have in America is highly superior to the Lada.

Our third day in Ekaterinburg was also a free day. We had to check out of the hotel at noon. Arkady was going to pick us up at 8:00 p.m.; our train for Omsk was leaving just after nine. I got out of bed at 6:30 a.m., dreading having to take another cold shower. I put my head under the hand-held shower and washed my hair. I faced the unpleasant task of the body wash. The cold water took my breath away. I quickly cut it off, soaped down, and discovered a small device on the wall from which I could hang the shower head. That I did, hoping to rinse off quickly. When the icy deluge of cold water hit me, I reacted, slipped, and fell out of the tub, which was about twice as high as tubs in our country. I couldn't grab anything; my shoulder and head hit the tile floor. For once I was glad I was hard headed, and I thanked the Lord for having looked after a physically inept individual. That was one of two hotels in which Andy and I had separate rooms. However, I knew if anything serious had happened to me, he would have found me very soon because it was about time for breakfast.

I saw Ena, an ex-Ekaterinburgian who lived in England, in the lobby, and we talked for a while. She mentioned that a Lada actually cost ten million rubles but that we would be surprised to see how many people were getting rich in Russia at the time and driving around in Mercedes 600s. Someone from Atlanta who had visited Russia a number of times commented on this. Evidently, just as in our country, those with real entrepreneurial skills and perhaps some money to launch a business were becoming successful, just like the carpet man in Estonia.

Andy and I took a taxi to a market. I was very weak, probably from not having eaten enough. We bought a banana and an apple and searched for a Coca-Cola but without success. We saw Snickers for $3.50 each; we had seen them elsewhere for 50¢ or $1, so we passed them up there.

Having finished perusing the market, we wanted to visit a department store. Andy saw a man who he said looked like a KGB agent, though the KGB didn't exist at that time. The man spoke to us, and we found out he was a businessman in a joint stock venture company doing export business. He offered us a ride to the department store. It took quite some time; evidently, it was far out of his way. His wife, who was very attractive, didn't speak English. He had a cellular telephone in his car. He treated us in the kind, considerate way so many other Russians had treated us.

We visited three or four stores, which were very uninteresting, but we did buy a heavy yardstick that I planned to whittle down with my Swiss knife given to me by my son-in-law, Jim Hill. I wanted to secure our door on the train with the stick so it couldn't be opened from the outside. It cost 16¢ in rubles—very inexpensive.

I couldn't find a place to exchange dollars for rubles. All the banks appeared to be closed. A black market ruble man gave me 1,014 rubles for a dollar, while the previous day, a bank had given Andy only 930 rubles for a dollar. I don't know why, but dollars were important to them. This same young man was very nice, spoke fairly good English, and was determined to come to America. He wanted to marry an American girl; that, of course, would give him an automatic entry into the United States. Andy and I liked him very much, but we refused to give him our address, though he sought it vigorously.

We caught a taxi back to the hotel and waited for Arkady to pick us up. He was a few minutes late, and we were a little worried, but there he was with his usual wide smile and happy attitude.

When we got to the train station, we discovered we had missed our train. That caused me some concern, but it was undue as it turned out. I had looked at the train tickets the night before and had read the departure time as 1930, but Arkady had read 2130, and a woman at the hotel also confirmed it was 2130, so I had given up though I had still been a tad suspicious. My suspicions had proven to be correct.

Arkady spoke no English, but he assured us everything would be okay. We don't know how he managed it, but within an hour, we were on a first-class train, just as our original train would have been, no problem. We were very grateful to Arkady, who had become quite a good friend.

The train ride to Omsk was uneventful and took far less time than we had been told in Atlanta it would take.

Omsk—Saturday, July 3, 1993

We accidently discovered that we were in Omsk at about 8:00 a.m. We were expecting a much later arrival and felt fortunate we hadn't gone on to the next stop as city arrivals were not announced. We grabbed our luggage and got off. Tanya, who was our Intourist representative, and a driver took us to the Hotel Irtysh, about five minutes away. Andy and I were most impressed with Intourist's ability to handle communications; evidently, Arkady followed through and let them know our time of arrival even though we'd missed the first train. That was certainly an impressive response. Andy and I had private rooms and some warm water that Saturday afternoon.

We had tremendous problems with Tanya when we tried to secure train tickets with the use of our vouchers. By using the book and a few words from other people who were in the lobby, we established our departure date, pickup time, and train departure time, and we left confident we would leave Omsk on time.

With great difficulty, we arranged a tour for the afternoon at $20 an hour. Tanya showed up with her daughter and Constantin, a Russian in his early twenties who spoke reasonably good English. As usual, we toured a cathedral, and Constantin indicated that there weren't many churches open in Russia those days. That was understandable after seventy years of atheism. Several Russians had asked Andy and me about our religion.

We visited a marketplace, and based on my memories of the farmers' markets I'd seen in my home city of Lynchburg, Virginia, in the early 1930s, the market was pre-1930s. We saw large jars of mixtures such as mayonnaise and country-cured meats that looked very much like our country-cured meats of yesterday and today. We saw some meat out in the open and sold under conditions that we had abandoned in our country fifty years earlier.

We had dinner at our hotel at five. It was most uninteresting, but we were able to eat it, and we caught a bus to the Irtysh River for a riverboat cruise.

Omsk, a city of 1.5 million, has two large rivers, the Omsk and the Irtysh. The Irtysh flows north for what looks like a thousand miles through Siberia to the Tara Sea. Andy and I were most impressed with the waterways in Russia, which has many large rivers as wide as or wider than the Mississippi.

We had difficulty getting tickets for the riverboat; we didn't know where to buy them. Finally, we were let aboard by a young man who spoke English. He had just graduated from a five-year institute where he had learned English. His name was Dema, and he was most pleasant and very personable. After the boat was underway on the Irtysh, Dema introduced us to Victor, an impressive young man who spoke even better English. We were joined by other young men, three of whom were named Igor, and a good-looking girl named Olga, and we had some great conversation with them.

Andrew was probably the most impressive, but he was somewhat drunk. They knew that we knew about their love of vodka and were apologetic about it. However, we went along with them, thinking they should celebrate this great occasion. We talked about Russia and America and religion. We had a lot of laughs with our group.

Victor was the most talkative and showed tremendous interest in the United States and our religion. Most people didn't seem involved whatsoever in religion, but the country was full of people furthering religion everywhere. The Billy Graham Crusades filled, I believed, the

Lenin Stadium in Moscow with people who were very interested in religion, and it can only grow in Russia. Omsk supposedly had only two churches open at the time.

The young group of graduates, one of whom showed us his diploma, were having a good time and were dancing. They seemed to make a habit of men dancing at times with men and women with women. Victor and Andrew motioned for me to dance with them, so I engaged in my first dance in Russia even though I'd told Andy I was going to dance with a Russian girl before returning home. They invited Andy and me to their table for vodka, but Andy declined. Their vodka was red; they had mixed it with cherry juice. I was supposed to drink it all in a gulp, but I let them know I couldn't do that. But it tasted pretty darn good, and we toasted each other. Our cruise on the Irtysh was interesting. People were on beaches even though it was past nine; the sun was still shining very brightly.

We left the boat, headed to our bus stop, and attempted to communicate with someone about the number of the bus we were supposed to take. A very happy woman who spoke no English understood what we were trying to do, as we had a note written by the hotel staff with its name and address. A woman came up to us; she spoke some English and showed us a postcard from her sister, who lived in Spartanburg, South Carolina. The woman taught the Bible to children in Omsk. The card from Spartanburg recognized the problems in Russia and wished them very much success during their rough times.

We asked the recent grads about the new system in Russia, and they, as was the case with everyone we had asked, weren't at all excited about it. We never seem to miss things we've never enjoyed. These people, who we believed had almost every kind of freedom they wanted, were unable to capitalize on it due to lack of capital and an entrepreneurial tradition and spirit.

Omsk had been a closed city; the Hotel Irtysh had been built strictly for the KGB. There weren't many hotels in any of the closed cities such as Ekaterinburg and Omsk. There was no tourism since tourists had never been permitted there, and only limited travel had been possible from these cities.

Omsk was somewhat more impressive than other cities we visited. The streets were in better shape, and though the city was old, its buildings didn't appear to be crumbling, as was the case in so many other areas. We even saw new construction; we caught sight of so many cranes everywhere. We laughed about there being a good crane salesman in Russia who sold his wares even when they had no use for them in most places.

The next morning, I arose at six thirty and let the hot water run for forty-five minutes before it got even close to what we would call lukewarm. Since we knew we'd have two days on the train without a bath, I decided to take a not-so-cold shower. It was not nearly as painful as the shower I had taken in Ekaterinburg. All hot water in the big cities was furnished from a central location, perhaps a power plant, and piped all over the city. As mentioned previously, the area of Ekaterinburg where we were was to be without hot water for the next month while the system was undergoing maintenance. We asked a few people about this; they all seemed to accept it without complaint. Everyone appeared clean, so they must have gotten used to cold baths.

Breakfast was impossible—a few small pieces of cheese, fatty prosciutto (Italian ham), and a bowl of something that looked like cottage cheese and was sweet. I couldn't eat anything, but Andy handled it all very well. I was embarrassed when the waitress saw I hadn't eaten, but I could have downed castor oil easier.

Tanya was right on time with her daughter and driver, but the driver was stopped on the way to the train station by a policeman, and an angry discussion ensued. We were unable to tell what was going on, but we felt perhaps he had been traveling the wrong route, and the argument didn't appear to be representative of the new Russia. The guide and her daughter took us right to the train car, went aboard, and took us to our compartment. What service!

It was a pretty day; Andy and I knew it was July 4. I was sad about missing July 4 in Atlanta with my neighbors. Sometime during the day, we toasted ourselves with peanut butter crackers, one pack of which Jane had forced into my suitcase at the last minute and for which I was glad.

Our second train trip in Siberia proved to be very much like the first. We saw mostly very flat country and had many stops along the way as we headed deeper into Siberia. Siberia was not what I had anticipated; it was very green all the way. We saw birch trees and many fir trees, though they were smaller than those in the States. It appeared that the forests had been cut, but many trees had been planted along the tracks perhaps to block the snow from covering them.

It wasn't unsettled country as we thought it would have been since Russia had probably controlled the growth of many cities. We stopped in Novosibirsk, a city of about two million. The country, with over 150 million people in the new Russia, had settlements just about every place along the Siberian railroad. All the villages looked about the same— old houses mixed with new construction. We thought people with money were doing something to the houses since private ownership was possible. Perhaps the people thought they would be able to live in the same place without government ownership.

We also saw lots of muddy roads leading into the woods and people working in large gardens. They were apparently growing much more than they could use for themselves. We wondered if their gardens had been as large in years past.

The next day, Monday, July 5, was another day of travel after a good night's sleep thanks to our security device on the door of our compartment. It was a nice day, and we were able to get off the train and enjoy twenty-minute stops for taking pictures.

We met Tony Wesolowsky, a young man from Philadelphia, whom I first thought was Russian. His American English accent was somewhat Russian, but we discovered his mother's and father's parents were Ukrainian. He had worked on the holocaust museum project in Washington for six months and had made many trips to this part of the world, including to former Eastern Europe satellite countries. He was extremely intelligent, and we enjoyed our conversations with him.

He was traveling alone and was planning to spend two nights in Irkutsk with a family who was going to charge him $40 per night. He was going from there to Mongolia to spend time with someone with whom he had made arrangements. He had been able to arrange his trip without paying the exorbitant price we had paid from the United States. His train ride from Moscow to Irkutsk cost him $38, and that included the second bed in his compartment because he wanted privacy.

He asked our train car attendant about her salary, and she told him she made 110,000 rubles, $110, per month, more than we have heard anyone making in Russia up to that point. That was perhaps the reason she could afford her gold teeth, which were very prominent in Russia. I'd noticed that Russians didn't have teeth as nice as Americans did because of our orthodontists.

Our lunch on the train the previous day consisted of cabbage soup, which was reasonably tasty but without much cabbage or potatoes. Dinner the previous night was a thin, overcooked, tough steak over rice. For breakfast, we had steak and rice much like the previous night's dinner. Andy skipped lunch; we ate some peanut butter crackers and shared a Hershey bar. I felt I had to eat something, so I went to lunch by myself and had steak again, but over potatoes, and it was edible.

The scenery was the best it had been since we had left Atlanta. This entire part of the world, from Warsaw to probably about two thousand miles east of Moscow, where we were then, had been almost entirely flat country—a hill here and there, but nothing comparable to the wonderful scenery in the mountains of our country or Germany, Switzerland, or Italy. We did see some beautiful rolling hills that reminded us of England, but we didn't see any mountains.

We stopped at a village, Krasnoyarsk, at about 9:00 a.m. and took pictures. The hills were more beautiful than we had seen before. Shortly after that, we crossed the Yenisey River. Our somewhat uneventful trip from Omsk to Irkutsk was over. We were ready for Irkutsk and Lake Baikal.

Irkutsk—July 6, 1993

We arrived in Irkutsk about 7:00 a.m. We were met by Intourist staff in a punctual manner and were taken directly to our hotel. We had been pleased by the ever-faithful Intourist and other travel agencies that always met us on time. They always managed to recognize us.

Irkutsk, a city of approximately eight hundred thousand that is about three hundred years old, is about thirty-two hundred miles east of Moscow. Its buildings and streets appeared to be in somewhat better condition than those in most of Russia. One must remember that in all areas of Russia, divided into regions, the top Communists there could have been better at getting things done, but generally, we saw very similar conditions, that is, infrastructure in need of much attention.

We were unfamiliar with the history of most of the cities we visited; we toured churches, museums, and other public places we would never hear about in the future. However, in almost all cases, we found points of interest and enjoyable people wherever we went.

We visited a four-hundred-year-old church, the only one we understood to be open in Irkutsk. We happened to encounter a priest who was effervescent in his communication to us about the history of the church. He took us throughout the church and showed us many things of which he was very proud. We saw a large book of gospels bound in metal—either brass, copper, or silver—that dated to 1648. He was obviously very proud of Russia.

We took an afternoon walk; we explored a large floating dry dock on the Angara River behind the hotel. We heard someone bathing in the river yell out, asking if we were Americans. Then came the words very clearly, "Do you speak English? F★★k you!" Whoever it was repeated himself a number of times. We decided we were in the wrong territory and reversed course; we made it back to the hotel without any problem.

We saw an Intourist truck that Andy and I estimated to be worth about $100,000. It was very beautifully done in quality fashion and serving as a concession in a park. The truck, which had been made in California, was another symbol of capitalism and entrepreneurship in Russia. We went there one evening to finish our eating.

Andy called Betty for about $5 a minute, expensive but worth it. We couldn't find a low-cost international telephone office in Irkutsk.

The next day, July 7, Andy and I were scheduled for a trip to Lake Baikal, the world's largest freshwater lake. It is about 400 miles long and between 18 and 50 miles wide. It's said to be about a mile deep in places and is purported to hold a sixth of the world's fresh water. It's filled by 336 rivers from Siberia and empties into the Angara River.

Natasha, our Russian guide, was in about her second year of studying English. She and her driver, Andrea, were in a Volga, just about the most prominent car in Russia if you need more space than a small Lada offers.

We had lunch at the southern tip of Lake Baikal and saw a hotel being renovated based on the carpenters and the crane we saw. I guessed it was capitalism at work; the place seemed to be in better condition than most places we had seen.

That afternoon, we found out why they were making the hotel look better. Boris Yeltsin and Helmut Kohl of Germany were supposed to have a conference there the next week. I wondered why they would be having a conference some thirty-two hundred miles from Moscow and much farther from Germany. We found out later that Yeltsin and Kohl were at a conference in Japan that President Clinton had attended and would be going home that way.

Fixing up the place for big honchos reminded me of the old National Cash Register (NCR) branch managers who would quickly clean up their places before visits from divisional vice presidents. I recalled chuckling at that and thinking no one should have to go to such extra effort. The roads we saw being repaved around the hotel were the first ones we saw in Russia undergoing such treatment. We saw herds of cows on the road that were not disturbed by automobiles or people; they stood their ground in the face of either.

I really wanted to see how families lived in the apartment complexes and in what looked like primitive villages. We saw cows in the yards, motorcycles with sidecars, no automobiles parked around the houses, and outhouses, all of which seemed to be the norm.

As we were walking with Natasha, I told her I'd give someone a thousand rubles if we could get in and see a house. Natasha quickly found a woman who lived in Irkutsk but owned a dacha, a Russian vacation or summer home, there. Hers was very crude even for a vacation home. Her husband had been dead for a few years; she said she was seventy-six. We went in and saw a large oven that reached up to the waist. It appeared to be concrete or some such hard substance on the outside and was very hot. She did her cooking and heated the place with it. Even though it was about seventy-five or so that day, she opened the door and pushed in some wood, making the place very hot. I guessed it made the place nice and toasty on cold Siberian nights.

The next room had three single beds covering three of the four walls. We took pictures, and we admired the woman's garden, in which she grew mostly potatoes, of course.

We saw a large statue of Lenin in Irkutsk though most other statues of Lenin had disappeared in Russia; Natasha couldn't explain that, but she spoke with respect for Lenin, whom during her school years they had called Grandpa Lenin. She said she had worn a red star in elementary school. I was somewhat enamored of Natasha and received a little kidding from Andy about that. Andy promised me he would destroy the video he had taken of us. I had some trouble figuring out if I'd be able to see the photos I took before Marie saw them and found out I'd been madly in love with Natasha. Marie would know I was kidding, but Natasha was very attractive and a fun person to be with.

We learned that Natasha couldn't have cared less for the new system under which they were living, as had been the case with most people we met in Russia.

I was tired of the food we had been eating even though Andy ate it without complaint. We decided to take a walk by the river and eat at the Intourist $100,000 concession truck. We took a long walk and noticed people fishing and a young couple drinking beer. I could just see the romance in the girl's eyes as she talked with her young man. We saw many children with dogs; we learned that dogs had not been very prevalent in Russia until recently and that it was currently popular to have dogs. We didn't try to communicate with any of them for fear they wouldn't understand us, and we couldn't afford shots for dog bites in Russia. I think that Andy and I, knowing that needles were reused in the country, would have headed home if we had to get a shot. We secured a Coke, I believe, and perhaps I had a beer at the Intourist counter along with crackers and a candy bar for dinner.

We were leaving the next day at 6:00 p.m. for a two-night and one-day trip to Ulan Bator in Mongolia. We took a boat cruise on the Angara River. After the cruise, we visited a museum near the river and saw interesting exhibits of what looked like our Indians and Eskimos. Alexander, a staff member at the museum, walked around with us. He pointed out that these were Bering Sea pictures, and I believe there was evidence that even our Indians came across the Bering Straits to America.

Alexander explained that he had taken English fifteen years earlier but hadn't talked to anyone who spoke English since then. He was somewhat difficult to understand, and he had difficulty understanding us; he would ask us to speak slowly. I assumed he wanted better enunciation than typical southerners often give. He was very politically minded and hated Boris Yeltsin. I cannot remember his exact words, but he indicated that he considered Yeltsin a buffoon and that Russia would never be anything with him in power. He believed Russia was close to civil war and that his children would never have anything.

Andy and I were very positive with everyone about the good things we thought would happen in Russia in the next few years, but Alexander was probably correct that it might take twenty years before he'd notice any difference. I think Russia, especially provincial Russia, is pre–1930s in so many ways. Only a very small percentage of people in the former Soviet Union knew of anything other than communism.

I read in the English version of the *Moscow Times*, which seemed to be a very independent newspaper, that America had ten times as many cars as did Russia. While we saw many cars on the streets, we almost never saw a traffic jam. Most women don't know how to drive, and so few cars are available that the masses just don't have the opportunity to drive. As I mentioned, we saw few cars even at the vast apartment complexes, the gigantic edifices to socialism in Russia.

That evening, a punctual Intourist took us to the railroad station and helped us board the train for the trip out of Russia to Mongolia.

Train to Ulan Bator—Thursday Night, July 8, 1993

We had a hard time understanding why the trip from Irkutsk straight down to Ulan Bator would take up to forty hours though it was only about two hundred and fifty miles away. We found out why when we boarded the train. We discovered we had to travel two hundred miles east to Ulan Ude and then take a train to Ulan Bator, the same distance as it would have been from Irkutsk.

Masses of people, more than we had seen before, were at the train station, and our train was loaded like a cattle car from stem to stern. We were supposed to have a hard sleeper with perhaps someone else in the room, but because of the wording on our voucher, Intourist was convinced we had paid for all four sleepers in our compartment. We were very surprised to run into our friend, Tony Wesolowsky, the Russian-speaking traveler from Philadelphia we had met on the train from Omsk to Irkutsk. Tony, not feeling very comfortable in a compartment with three others, asked if he could stay with us. Andy and I agreed that it would be a good deal for us too considering Tony's ability with the language.

Andy and I fought our way through about ten cars on our weaving train, people every step of the way, to the dining car. We ordered about the only thing available, beefsteak and soup, and were joined by two

Mongolians who appeared to be very nice. A third sat on the knee of another at our table. They soon left, and a young Mongolian married couple showed up and had dinner with us, but we were unable to communicate with them.

Before noon on the next day, Friday, we understood that we would be stopping for about four hours before we reached the Mongolian border. That turned out to be more like eight hours; the train shifted cars back and forth and swapped the Russian electric locomotive for a Mongolian diesel locomotive. During all that time, we were without food because the dining car was closed, and we had no drinking water or hot water to make coffee, and we had no toilet.

By the time we crossed the Mongolian border, perhaps fifteen minutes or so to the customs station, we had another wait of between two to four hours. I was getting upset and uncomfortable with the delays, but we could do nothing about it.

We left the train and walked to a small village area where we saw a memorial to those who had died in World War II. Though we saw only twenty-four names inscribed on the tomb, we realized they hadn't forgotten the deeds of those men or would forget the perpetrators.

Ulan Ude in southern Russia was a much more sparsely populated area with rolling hills and a somewhat rougher terrain, much like the extreme northern part of Mongolia.

We saw many hills and valleys but fewer trees in the beautiful Mongolian countryside. The hills reminded me of those around San Diego going up to San Francisco. It was a rainy time of year, and everything was a gorgeous green. Everything looked like grassland populated by many sheep and cattle and horse herders. The Mongolian people are considered nomadic; we saw many herds and the yurts that provide the housing for the herdsmen. We got the feeling this was the way they had been living for centuries.

Yurts, called *gers* in some publications, are round, tentlike structures with stoves in the center, bedding around the side, and places to sit; they appear very neat from the outside. They are quickly collapsed and moved from place to place as the herds move to new grazing lands. Supposedly, the herdsmen can move any place they want to as long as they find grass. Early Saturday morning, we saw horsemen in fast trots and traveling close to the train as well as in distant fields. It was my introduction to the Mongolians' love for horses. The countryside was magnificent; it had more of a vacation atmosphere than anything we had seen thus far beginning in Warsaw.

Since the train was so crowded, the conductor or attendant requested that someone else use the vacant bunk in our compartment on Friday night, but we refused. During the night, we heard a loud banging at the door and a voice that was probably saying, "Open the door." We refused to do so. The lock turned with the common key that would have enabled access to our compartment. However, since we were using the device invented by the genius Andy Anderson, the person couldn't move the door even a fraction of an inch. We remained in our bunks and continued without further interruption during the night.

We experienced another unusual incident on Friday. Andy had videoed the customs agents at the Mongolian border, and apparently, they had noticed it and objected to it. Later, while I was guarding the compartment, a customs agent showed up, saw the video camera, and asked me, I thought, to open the camera. When I didn't, he asked for my passport, stuck it in his pocket, and started to leave. I knew that if he left with my passport, I could have had a very serious problem. I held onto his arm and asked Tim, a seven-foot German youngster on his way to the Gobi Desert, to find Andy fast. Andy hurried back in and didn't accede to the customs agent's request to give up the film in the camera. I got my passport back, but the customs agent took Andy's passport and left the train. Fast-thinking Andy hurriedly switched the tape in the video camera with a blank tape and rushed after the agent. Tony went along with him. I was watching through the window, knowing we'd be stranded without Andy's passport. A few other people joined Andy to criticize the customs agent for his actions. The train started to leave, and I thought we were in real trouble. However,

Andy returned with his passport. Thank goodness for Tony, our unpaid interpreter.

On Saturday morning, before we arrived in Ulan Bator, Andy noticed several Mongolians in our car punching it out among themselves. One had a bloody nose, someone was choking someone, and so on. With that going on, and with the filthy toilets and other discomforts, it was a real pleasure to arrive in Ulan Bator and meet Bataar, our guide, right after getting off the train. We were checking in at the hotel in ten minutes.

For our four days in Ulan Bator, we were provided with a full-time guide, a driver, and a brand-new Volga with only 900 kilometers, 500 miles on it. Bataar ate every meal with us and stayed with us night and day if we desired his presence. He was extremely nice, and we liked him very much, but he had some problems with communications since he had had only two months of English. For instance, he told us that an extra price we would have to pay to go into the countryside would be $17, but when we arrived, we found out the price was actually $70. We decided not to take the trip at that price, but we were fortunate the next day to get quite a distance into the country and see many villages.

We had ridden in Volgas every place we had visited with guides. It's a four-cylinder car that's not quite as well put together as the '50 six-cylinder Chevy I owned. We looked at the engine; it was very small and had very little power. It was reasonably stylish, but the workmanship was very poor inside; we saw vinyl and other things that didn't appear to be new. The carburetor was inferior; many times, the car started very poorly, and its exhaust system rattled. But evidently, it was a fairly durable car. We were told that the price was $6,000, which we thought was unbelievable, but we knew there had been no engineering and development put into it since its inception. The price conflicted with what we'd been told a Lada would cost—from $8,000 to $10,000, but you'll get a range of opinions even in America when you ask people what something costs. Someone said a Lada could run $12,000.

The Hotel Bayangol provided the nicest room we had had so far on our trip, complete with American plumbing fixtures and a shower attached to the wall. The bathtub was about two-thirds as long as ours. It was going to be a pleasure to have hot water again, but we soon discovered that all the hot water, which came from the local power plant, had been used up. My shower wasn't cold enough to knock me off my feet, but it wasn't even lukewarm. However, after that, we had hot showers each morning by getting up early.

We visited a hillside with a memorial to the Mongolian Revolution, which occurred in 1921, four years after the Bolshevik Revolution. It was a beautiful monument with an engraved head of Lenin and many symbols and an engraving of Stalin, which was most unusual to see in any place we had been. It was a tribute to him for the Great War, 1941–45.

Ulan Bator is a city of over a half million; the country has 2.2 million people and 25 million animals, including large herds of sheep, horses, and cattle. We were told they had 8 million horses, and when we said that was about four horses per person, Bataar said, "Yes, but the reason we have so many is we eat the horses." He assured us, however, that we were not eating any horsemeat at the hotel restaurant.

The city was much nicer looking than most former Soviet cities or satellite countries; we were impressed. But as usual, we saw parks and grassy areas that were way overgrown. No one had been able to explain this to us; we decided it was probably due to a shortage of funds. No one really seemed to understand our surprise at that; we assumed it was the lack of attention given to so many things in this part of the world.

Bataar told us on two separate days that the rainfall in the area was 250 centimeters annually, and I figured that was about one inch. In retrospect, one inch is closer to 2.5 millimeters, and I question whether this is correct. However, the area around Ulan Bator was extremely dry, and we saw no agriculture. We noticed later that when we headed back north in Mongolia toward Russia, agriculture and gardens and even large farms began almost immediately.

We happened to arrive in Ulan Bator during an annual celebration, the Naadam Festival, which had been going on for several centuries, but beginning with the 1921 revolution, it became a tribute to the freedom of Mongolia and its turn to communism. We saw the president of Mongolia at the opening ceremonies at the stadium and watched the first round of wrestling matches. The wrestling was different from what we had seen in the United States; two wrestlers pulled and shoved at each other until one hit the ground. The 1,024 wrestlers in the first round weren't matched in height or weight.

One day, we traveled about ten or fifteen miles into the countryside to view horse races. We saw horses in the distance coming over a hill in single file. The final number was supposed to be about two hundred for the race. It was beautiful, but unfortunately, all spectators had to remain about a half mile away. The Mongolians truly love horses; it seemed that everybody had come out for these races.

In the early evening, we saw a wonderful Mongolian-style concert, complete with colorful costumes, instruments we had never seen before, and the kind of singing that sounded impossible for anyone to produce with just vocal chords. Andy tried recording the concert, but he was told to stop about halfway through.

We traveled about twenty miles into the countryside and saw trees and low, rolling mountains. We spotted the first wild animals we'd seen on the trip—a herd of about twenty deer with three or four bucks. We went up the hill and approached them; they were very tame and didn't move. They were beautiful animals. We learned that during the winter, they come down to the city to eat. They were decreed untouchable by law.

We attended the last days of the wrestling sessions and encountered a severe rainstorm with hail. The wrestling stopped, and the rain continued for quite some time, so we left for dinner at the hotel. I went to the room, while Andy, with his excessive energy, toured a park with Bataar and visited with many guests in the huge dining room of the hotel.

On Tuesday, our last day in Mongolia, we took a drive into the country perhaps as much as twenty-five miles and saw many impoverished villages. I saw no gardens, but I believe Andy spotted one or two. We saw no stores. Bataar said these people had to go into the city to get their food. Since they didn't have gardens, we wondered how they survived.

We walked a hilly area and saw a children's summer camp. It was closed that summer because the water lines had frozen the previous winter and hadn't been repaired. We were told that children had to pay to attend the camp. It was very much in disrepair and needed much more work than just the water system.

We saw a herdsman who was evidently a security guard for the camp. He had a herd of fifteen goats. The male goat wore a chastity belt. Evidently, he was too active at the wrong time, and this method was used to discourage him from engaging in sexual harassment or unauthorized sex.

The herdsman invited us into the walled complex. We wanted to take pictures of him and his yurt, but he wouldn't permit it. We looked around the camp, and responding to his friendly attitude, went inside his yurt. We were very glad we were able to do that. He claimed that he had a son in India, another in Japan, two daughters who were doctors in Ulan Bator, and two other children. He said he had a brother who had bought a Russian manufacturing plant for $3 million. Bataar felt he might have been exaggerating, especially since he appeared to be a little intoxicated. His face was leathery as other Mongolians' faces were due to the severe weather. He was more than hospitable. He dipped into a large leather pouch on the wall and withdrew a dipperful of a clabbered substance that we were told was cream. He filled a bowl and invited us to participate. We refused even though we were concerned he might be offended. He showed no negative reaction, however. He took out a bottle of vodka and wanted us to join him. We asked Bataar to tell him it was against our religion, hoping that he would understand why we didn't accept his graciousness. It was a great visit, and when everybody's back was turned, I took a picture on the outside.

That afternoon, we visited temples, and we encountered two nice American girls traveling together from Minnesota and California who spoke Russian. One was going to school in Warsaw and the other in the Czech Republic. We also ran into a French girl who spoke beautiful English and was traveling alone even though she spoke neither Russian nor Mongolian. She had China and Tibet included in her trip, but she thought Tibet had been closed by the Chinese for visits by foreigners at the time.

We stopped in a department store that was typical for former Communist countries; it was very sparsely stocked with merchandise; so many enclosed departments were selling so few items that we wondered how they could justify a salesperson. Bataar told us the goods were very expensive. A cashmere sweater was priced at $60. Bataar wanted to know if I thought that was expensive, and I told him it looked like a good price for a cashmere sweater. He said it was very expensive for them; the average Mongolian made about $50 a month. We had some doubt about that, as it conflicted with other information we had received, but at least it was an opinion and possibly a fact. It was, however, obvious that Mongolians, especially those in the countryside, were poor.

We saw a large Ferris wheel and other amusements for children in one park, but again, the place was overgrown—nothing like the parks in our country.

Ever since I had started planning this trip, I was perplexed about the Russian influence in Mongolia, knowing that Mongolia was not a part of the Soviet Union but that it was Communist. I always thought Mongolians would relate more to the Chinese than to the Russians. It was also strange to me that Mongolians would use the Cyrillic alphabet that's used in Russia.

Prior to the 1921 revolution, which was influenced by Russia, Mongolia wasn't permitted to assume its independence by either China or Russia. With the revolution, Mongolia claimed its independence and evidently became very attached to the Soviet Union. Ulan Bator, the capital, is within two hundred miles of the Russian border and probably five hundred miles from the Chinese border. Bataar indicated that the Mongolians didn't like the Chinese.

Statues of Lenin—and I believe I recall one of Stalin—had been pulled down after 1990, indicating also the country's break with communism. One would have to assume that every country that broke with the Soviet Union had realized long before then that communism didn't work and grasped the first opportunity to disassociate themselves and make the radical change to a democratic form of government.

Juulchin, the tourist agency in Ulan Bator, was an example of free enterprise. Prior to 1990, it was a state-run agency. The director told us that it was at the time owned by seven thousand stockholders. We were impressed with the new equipment they had, including new vans and computers. The manner in which the agency was managed was impressive; the top man there gave us much attention. It was evident that capitalism was at work and introduced something to this society in Mongolia with which almost no one was familiar.

When people are exposed to capitalism and communism and have witnessed firsthand the differences between motivated management and employees and those under communism who have little personal incentive, they denounce socialism.

Food at the hotel was good—not the quality of American food, but we always had several courses, including soup and dessert, with each meal. We were satisfied with the quality of the food especially compared to meals we'd had on most of the trip.

Our train was departing at 7:00 p.m., and Bataar, who had purchased our tickets, took us to the train and directly to our compartment. He said we would arrive the next morning, which we didn't believe. That was corrected; we learned we'd arrive the next night at about ten, about twenty-seven hours total.

Ours was a second-class train; there were four beds in each compartment. We made ourselves comfortable in ours, having paid $60 extra for the two upper berths so we wouldn't have to share the compartment. But then we discovered Tony was on the same train and again invited him to share our compartment.

On the night of July 14, we settled in for the night. I awoke several times as I did at home. Between four and five the next morning, the train stopped. We endured the usual two- to three-hour customs check leaving Mongolia and then a six- to eight-hour check going back into Russia. While we had a total of four or five cars leaving Ulan Bator, with other trains making connections to ours, we must have ended up with fifteen or more cars. It was a somewhat uneventful trip, perhaps since we were taking the same route back to Ulan Ude.

About four that afternoon, Andy and I ate baked chicken and noodle soup in the dining car. The meals in all the dining cars consisted of soup and chicken or beef and potatoes, and they were usually inexpensive. We always have a hard time getting hot chai, tea, at the beginning of the meal. It looked like they didn't understand, or maybe they were lazy about serving.

Ulan Ude—Wednesday, July 14, 1993

We got to Ulan Ude about 10:00 p.m. and were met by Svetlana from Intourist and her driver. She was upset because she had made the trip earlier to the train station and discovered we were probably going to be on a later train. Ulan Bator hadn't notified her. That was the first time such miscommunication had happened. However, she was on time, and as usual, Intourist's service impressed Andy and me. We checked into the Hotel Geser and settled in for the evening, looking forward to a hot shower the next morning.

Almost all restaurants in Russia open at 8:00 a.m., which I consider to be the middle of the day for businesspeople. We were anxious to have breakfast and meet our guide at nine. While trying to order a buffet-style breakfast, we met Julia, a woman whose English was excellent. She assisted us in ordering and was very understanding. She was good looking also. She had been living in Seattle for about two years and was the fiancée of an American businessman who had traveled to Russia. We met him when he and Julia were having breakfast and discovered he was about twenty years her senior. Andy and I hoped it was true love and not just an automatic ticket to America and the good life.

During breakfast, we met an American banking consultant who was under US government auspices, offering services to improve cooperative banking. He was somewhat more negative about Russia than Andy and I had been; we had tried to be very open minded and understanding, but he was close to being correct in his evaluation of incompetency in Russia as well as the lack of motivation and desire to do things well.

We met Nadia, our tour guide, and traveled about fifteen miles in the country to see the headquarters of the Buddhist religion in Russia. It was in a very worn-out village that had been in existence for about forty years. We learned it had come about as a result of President Eisenhower suggesting to Stalin that he open up the Buddhist religion. I wondered what interest Eisenhower had had in Buddhism.

Our driver was somewhat of a maniac on the road; I doubted he would live long as he passed everything on the highway without looking to see what was in front or what he might encounter along the way.

In the city of Ulan Ude, we saw many wooden houses that had been built after a fire that had wiped out most of the old wooden houses built prior to 1878. They were built of very sturdy logs. Nadia pointed out the "worst" house in Ulan Ude; it had been the NKVD headquarters and later the KGB headquarters. NKVD was the predecessor of KGB. I recalled the change and remembered it had taken place to change the image of the NKVD. Hatred for the KGB was universal in Russia. Nadia told us that people had been slaughtered in the basement in unbelievable manners, and we could tell she was serious about it.

Nadia asked us about lunch, and we let her choose the place. We went to what I recall was the Ministry of Russian Affairs and had a very low-cost, cafeteria-style lunch. I had a couple of what I called dumplings, meat wrapped in a pastry and either fried or baked. I found it to be inedible, much to my embarrassment.

Nadia and Svetlana arranged for two teenage youngsters to take us to the train station and get us on the train. They were inexperienced in locating the train and so forth, but we made out okay. They were very friendly, and we liked them. We hoped the two young guys would reap their rewards in the years ahead that a free Russia, with so many opportunities opening up, would provide.

Trans-Siberian to Khabarovsk—
Thursday, July 15, 1993

The train to Khabarovsk was supposed to take just over fifty hours; we were to spend two nights on the train as we traveled about fifteen hundred miles. We boarded and met Maria, our car attendant or conductor. She was a very hospitable woman with a huge smile and many gold teeth, a prominent mark of cosmetic improvement in Russia.

It was obvious that it was going to be a very friendly train ride after we met a number of people who were going all the way to Vladivostok. Nicholas and his wife, Nadia, were the first people we met. Nicholas had served time in the Russian navy, and when I asked him what kind of ship he had been on, he answered "Many ships." I wasn't sure if he wanted to convey that information. However, he was friendly and told us he had been working in banking since retiring from the navy. His residence had always been in Vladivostok, while Nadia was from Yaroslavl, very close to Moscow.

We also met a Lutheran minister named Heinz, from Hanover, Germany. He pointed out in a very friendly and enthusiastic manner that we had better take a picture of Lenin's bust as it would likely be the last time we would see it as it was coming down. He was joking, and I wondered if Nicholas would take offense, but evidently, Nicholas agreed with him.

We also met Catherine, from Paris, who was about thirty, and her interpreter and guide, Yuri, from Moscow. Yuri spoke excellent English and proved to be a very interesting person to whom I could talk about situations in the old Soviet Union and today's new Russia.

Our journey to Khabarovsk would take over forty-eight hours and would be the longest train ride so far, putting us about fifty-five hundred miles from Moscow with roughly three hundred to go on the next leg to Vladivostok after two nights in Khabarovsk.

Shortly after we departed Ulan Ude, we found ourselves in a somewhat mountainous part of Siberia compared to other areas we had seen in the flat country. We photographed some very beautiful scenes, and Andy videotaped many interesting sites.

Almost all Russians describe Siberia as a dry part of the country with a short growing season and harsh, frigid winters. While Siberia isn't as far north as are the Scandinavian countries, it isn't near the Gulf Stream, as is Norway, which would be very frigid and possibly uninhabitable without the Gulf Stream. The Siberia I saw was green; there must have been enough water that year, but the trees were small. We didn't know if the trees were naturally small or if they had been planted after older trees had been harvested, but a short growing season doesn't produce fast-growing timber.

We saw many lumber mills along the way, many of them very large. An American we met in the Hotel Geser, Julia's fiancé actually, was in the timber-buying business, and Siberia has as much timber as perhaps any country. We also saw very large logs on railroad cars that we guessed were from the interior and many years old. On the second day, we saw hilly terrain and some extensive green plains.

Andy and I had different opinions about the agriculture we saw. When we saw villages and signs of residential life, we also saw huge potato gardens; it looked like potatoes were the only thing raised in peasant villages. Potatoes were stored underground as a way of preserving them from rotting.

I thought that Russia wasn't as able to feed itself at that time as well as the Soviet Union had fed itself even three years earlier. In my opinion, the good growing seasons would be in the southern republics that were no longer parts of the old Soviet Union. Ukraine, the breadbasket of the Soviet Union, played a vital part in feeding Russia, so that meant Russia had to import huge amounts of agricultural products from there. For the most part, I'd seen only potatoes being grown, but that day, we saw gardens also growing cabbages and sunflowers. Andy said he had seen green beans but not in abundance.

We stopped at a town and visited a farmers' market. We saw beautiful beets two or three inches in diameter, small carrots, potatoes of course, onions that looked good with their tops still on, and raspberries. Many on the train purchased the raspberries.

Andy bought a very appetizing looking roll and a fried something or other for lunch. Andy liked it; I ate one but didn't care for it. I believe it had eggs stuffed in it. We bought six or eight boiled potatoes for 30¢, and I ate most of them. They were good even without salt and pepper. Black pepper was almost unavailable; when it was, it would be served on a small dish; diners would pinch some and put it on their food. Andy was greatly surprised when he saw me pinching pepper from an open container. When I thought about the dirty fingers that had been there before mine, I refrained from any further consumption of pepper. Salt was served in the same manner. Many people put salt on the end of a knife and tapped it over their food. Salt and pepper weren't served that way in restaurants. Most of the pepper served in restaurants was a red, very hot pepper I assumed was cayenne.

Food on the train was less than satisfactory as usual. Most of the dining cars on the trains served potatoes and beef or chicken and sometimes rice, accompanied by a borscht with cabbage or potatoes. In most cases, it was edible. Bread was the same throughout Russia— brown or brown and white. O how I longed for a Hungry Jack ! Andy and I stayed away from the dining car for breakfast; we made coffee with the hot water that was always available on first-class trains and a rolled cake we had bought on the side of the tracks at one of our stops.

On Saturday, we saw more mountainous terrain and some beautiful streams. I don't want to detract from Siberia's beauty, but it wasn't as beautiful as what I had expected. Andy shared the feeling, I believed. It was surprising to us that in all the miles we had traveled in Siberia and Mongolia, we had seen only one wild animal, a gray fox Andy had sighted in Mongolia. I failed to take pictures on our return trip from Mongolia, but the terrain near the Russian border was beautiful and about as pretty as we had seen at any time.

I became somewhat lazy in adding to the few words I knew in Russian but enjoyed a book my daughter, Susan, had given me that supplemented one that I had purchased on the Russian language. Her book on Moscow was very good, and another on Moscow and Leningrad was also good; they enabled us to learn something about each place we visited, and they gave us more information than was available in Fodor's.

Thinking about eating and drinking, Andy tried mares' milk (a female horse for those city slickers who may not understand what a mare is) during the Naadam Festival in Mongolia. Our guide, Bataar, bought this and relished it, but I couldn't make myself taste it.

At that point, I needed a good bath, not having had one for two and a half days. I had brought along an electric razor, but I decided to rough it and look like a part of the real Siberia before arrival in Khabarovsk. It also made me look like a professional train rider.

Quite a few interesting things happened on that leg of our trip; one passenger was robbed by his apartment mate the first night. He was from a large church in Hanover, but he hit the bottle considerably. That surprised us. He had been wearing a moneybag, but when he awoke, his money, camera, and glasses were missing. He borrowed some rubles from Nicholas until he got to Vladivostok where he thought he could cash some travelers' checks.

Only because of Andy's special invention had we felt secure while sleeping. The train was noisy; we had only a slim chance of hearing anyone enter our compartment. These trains appear to be full of thieves, and everyone was wary of them. Andy and I somewhat dreaded the trip to Moscow to Odessa; we knew it would be a second-class train with a hard sleeper, meaning two others would sleep in the compartment with us. Perhaps we would rent the two additional beds as we had on the trip to Ulan Ude to keep ourselves safe from robbers.

Nicholas was very friendly, as were Yuri and Catherine. Nicholas invited us to call him when we got to Vladivostok; he would do anything to help us. We told him that our two nights in Vladivostok might turn out to be only one, which wouldn't give us any time for visiting. We got his address because he wanted a copy of a picture taken of all of us sent to him in Vladivostok.

We had an interesting experience on the train with of all things an abacus. The dining car attendant produced two sets of identical figures; he wanted to test his speed against Andy's calculator. He beat Andy hands down. I remembered that when our NCR cash register salesmen encountered abacuses thirty or forty years ago, they would lose to the abacus.

I mentioned earlier that I thought Russia was in the 1930, but it was actually in the 1920s based on the way things were still being done. The abacus was used almost everywhere, and tape isn't used to wrap packages. Rather, the wrapping is folded and tucked into itself. When people go shopping for food or anything else for that matter, they bring along bags for their purchases, including meat.

We saw some progress in cutting hay and preserving it for future use in the field. We saw large rolls over a massive area that was probably a collective farm; it seemed to encompass several square miles. It was rolled just as we do it today in the United States.

Toward the end of the day, when we were within a couple of hours of Khabarovsk, I happened to walk with Nicholas to Gennady's compartment. Gennady was a hunter. He was at least seven feet tall and was very handsome. He had venison spread out on his table with vodka and other juices and edibles. Gennady insisted, in Russian, that I eat with them and celebrate. Nicholas insisted that everything was okay. The smoked venison or deer meat was delicious; it was one of the tastiest foods I'd had since Atlanta. This was followed by vodka that had some cherry juice mixed in. I sipped it even though Gennady wanted me to down a whole shot. We had a great time, but since the party was becoming somewhat "festive" and Nicholas was constantly having to push Heinz away from him, I thought it was a good time to leave. The Hanoverian Lutheran minister, with a 2,000-member congregation, drank excessively. He had begun pushing on Nicholas in an aggravating manner for no reason. Previously, Andy had seen Nicholas's wife slap him on both sides of his face when Nicholas was not present. Andy didn't know exactly what he had done.

Let me say something about my associate on this trip. I gained insight into the inventive, inquisitive mind of Andy "Thomas Alva Edison" Anderson. Andy has to know how everything works. He saw things in Russia that no other American had ever seen. He inspected and dismantled a variety of toilet water closets, had persistently tried to repair a leaky one but had failed, and he came up with the ingenious device to ensure our security in our train compartments.

He inspected everything from the top stories and floors of our hotels with attempts to get on the roof. That morning, he videoed the changing of a brake shoe that had gotten hot and had been discovered by the "tire kickers" who went down tapping boxes on the train's undercarriage. They changed the defective brake shoe in minutes. They just threw another one in place, and through the ingeniousness of Russian engineering, it required no external devices other than its own mechanism to hold it in place. My hat's off to Andy, and I hope that sometime he will merit the awards of Thomas Alva himself. There is one thing about him that is lacking—he's not able to catnap during the day and sleep very few hours at night like Thomas Alva and myself.

I didn't understand the way Russians named themselves. For instance, I thought that Nicholas's last name was Pavlovsky. However, in securing his full name and address, I found his name to be Nicholas Netedova. Pavlovsky, which he had been using, was evidently his middle name. I received an explanation about this but never fully understood the different usages.

As we arrived in the Khabarovsk railroad station, Nicholas and Heinz insisted that they help us get our baggage off the train. Standing on the ground, Nicholas asked if he could make a recording on my tape. He said, "I wish you from my country, to your good house, their success, and good health for you and your children. Thank you." My reply was, "Thank you, Nicholas. You are a good friend, and we will remember you and Russia."

We shook hands many times with the whole crowd and started looking for Intourist. Unable to locate our Intourist person, we took the baggage to the front of the railroad station and waited. Andy decided to look around while I guarded the baggage. Andy soon returned, and I went to see if I could find the Intourist representative. I returned to Andy and saw someone I thought was the Intourist person talking enthusiastically to Andy. Discovering that he was not Intourist, and being a little bit suspicious of anyone else taking us to the hotel, not knowing where we might end up, I suggested we look for an official taxi.

I went over to look for a yellow taxi and heard Andy yell, "Roy!" I thought Intourist had arrived, but he told me his large bag, packed for fifty-two days, was missing. I was shocked. That was worse than losing all our money. I took a fast look around and ran back through the station, but no one was around. Andy thought about the things of value that were gone, including video tapes of everywhere we had been, including Mongolia. It was a serious loss for us; the tapes provided graphic descriptions of the landscapes we had seen and the people we had met.

We got a taxi to the Hotel Intourist in Khabarovsk. The male Intourist representative, who spoke excellent English, was very disturbed at our loss. It wouldn't have happened if someone from Intourist had met us. Having experienced Murphy's Law during my many years in business and the failure of so many people to follow through, I wasn't surprised that Intourist, which we had bragged about so much, had finally failed us.

Khabarovsk—Sunday, July 18, 1993

We planned to take a two-hour tour on Sunday. Nadia, our interpreter, was accompanied by Alexander, Sasha for short, in his Toyota van. That was the first time we'd been in a foreign- made vehicle.

Khabarovsk is a city of either six or seven hundred thousand people, depending upon whom you ask. It was one of the nicest cities we had visited in Russia. Perhaps we were getting accustomed to run-down buildings. The wide streets were lined with many trees and were in relatively good repair. Maybe that was because there were few streetcars whose tracks made it harder to keep the streets in repair because of not being able to keep putting asphalt above the tracks.

We visited Lenin Square and saw a statue of Lenin. We also saw the White House, a large, beautiful building of Russian marble used extensively in almost every building. It had been the original Communist headquarters and served the democratic system as the Khabarovsk region's governmental headquarters.

The city was about fifty-four hundred miles from Moscow on the Amur, the second-largest river in Russia. It seemed in most places to be much larger than the Mississippi, and we saw many ships on it. Andy and I were impressed by the amount of shipping we saw on Russia's large rivers.

We saw a large statue of the city founder; I've forgotten his first name though I was able to read it with confirmation by Nadia, thinking that I would remember it. It was an impressive statue.

We were told we could visit the Chinese border. Wanting to see China even at a distance, we took a fifteen-mile trip to the border. The border was closed, but traffic was coming both ways, and we saw an island in the Amur River but not China. Nadia and Sasha took us on a fifteen-minute drive to a place we could see Chinese territory, and then we returned to our hotel.

Intourist felt bad about the stolen luggage and gave us a free boat ride on the Amur River. We enjoyed the trip and met quite a few Americans from all over the States who had gotten to Khabarovsk on Alaskan Air Lines. Later that evening, Intourist treated us to a free concert. Andy and I enjoyed listening to two beautiful, young Russian sopranos.

The next day, we walked for miles before we found an adequate piece of luggage for Andy. We stopped at an international telephone center but found it didn't have connections to the United States on Mondays. We stopped at another exchange, but it as well had no connections to the United States on Mondays. The assumption was that lines were too busy on Mondays with business use.

We ate at a new Japanese restaurant and had apple juice and crab meat salads, the first crab meat we had seen, and it was good. We encountered a new way of payment at a restaurant; after we ordered, we had to leave the table and pay the cashier before the food was served. We ordered something additional, and we had to go through the same routine. It was unusual for Japanese to do business in that manner.

Back at the hotel, I gave Andy some of my clothes, having brought along a bunch. We were reasonably well fixed for clothes for the rest of the trip without having to do much laundry. I must say that Andy looked like a real he-man in my clothes.

At 9:00 p.m., we met Intourist for a trip to the train station and departure for Vladivostok. Sasha was again our driver, and he bent over backward to keep us from having to wait in the station very long, as he had been instructed by Intourist. He took us aboard the train and helped us with our luggage as usual.

Our uneventful trip to Vladivostok took about eleven hours. We met Pita, a Russian, and his wife, Lena, his son Vatilia, and a younger son I think was named Denis. They spoke very little English, but Denis, who appeared to be about ten, was evidently learning the language. He gave us many big smiles and spoke some English very well.

Vladivostok—Tuesday, July 20, 1993

Svetlana, an Intourist agent with very good English, met us in Vladivostok and took us to our hotel. We were signed up for two nights in the Hotel Vladivostok but discovered when looking at our voucher for the plane ticket that we were to leave in twenty-four hours, at 2:50 p.m. Wednesday afternoon. Fortunately, we discovered this; Svetlana had wanted to wait until the next day to get the plane tickets since she had no experience in acquiring tickets for anyone.

Vladivostok was a closed city until September 1992, so it was without any kind of tours or tour agents as far as we could determine. We tried to arrange a tour with Svetlana, but she was unable to do so. However, she did get our plane tickets for Moscow.

We were planning to go downstairs to see if we could line up a guide to the city when the telephone rang. It was Catherine from Paris and Yuri. We met them in the lobby and started for a walk about three thirty. Our walk lasted until about eight or nine that evening, and then we had dinner together. The total dinner for the four of us, including caviar and appetizers for Yuri and Catherine and a carton of wine from Spain, cost $14.25. Except for places priced in dollars with international menus for travelers, Russian restaurants were very inexpensive.

Andy and I were anxious to see navy ships. We saw quite a few ships in the very deep harbor, which appeared to be enclosed by hills and mountains. We were fairly certain we saw at least two cruisers and some destroyers but couldn't recognize the destroyers for a certainty. We could see the Sea of Japan in the distance. We saw what appeared to be another heavily armed cruiser within a couple of hundred feet from us and other navy ships. The number of navy ships was not as large as I had anticipated, considering Vladivostok was the base for the Russian navy's Pacific fleet. Perhaps a good number of ships were at sea.

We also saw the usual war memorial, but this one had been constructed much differently from those we have seen previously as a tribute to the Great War of 1941–45. The Russians did great jobs on their monuments and were very proud of their World War II victory. At the monument, we saw a large submarine of the conventional type that was housed on stands and used as a navy museum. Andy and I saw torpedo firing mechanisms and torpedoes much as the submarine would have used in war.

At the hotel, we met Charlotte, a German in her fifties who spoke good English. She had been born in Germany, was married to an Englishman, and lived in Hong Kong. She had traveled to Vladivostok by herself on a ferry and was going to take tours from Vladivostok, arranged by herself, north of the Siberian railroad to Yakutsk and other places.

We also met Donata, who was in her early twenties, but only for a few minutes; we were not sure of her itinerary.

Charlotte, Charlotta in German, took us on a downtown tour that helped us route our way just in case we couldn't find a tour guide. We stayed with her a couple of hours and had coffee with her. When she returned to the hotel, we remained on our own tour for a while and returned to the hotel for a three thirty appointment with Svetlana.

About 11:00 p.m., when Yuri and Catherine were visiting us, a call came to the room. Yuri answered the phone and indicated that it was a woman who wanted to talk to him or me when we were alone. She said she would call back later. She did call later, and we figured out she was a prostitute. I couldn't get rid of her pleasantly, so I told her I'd let her talk to my wife. I gave the phone to Catherine. Our caller decided to hang up.

The next day, we had little time to do anything because our driver was picking us up at twelve thirty for a one-hour drive to the airport and our two fifty flight to Moscow. Catherine and Yuri came over to take showers about eleven; they were very grateful for our hot water since evidently they had only cold water where they were staying.

Just before Yuri and Catherine came, Andy was out videoing, and I failed to lock the door as we normally did. The door opened, and a uniformed person came through accompanied by a civilian in coat and tie. I was startled, thinking that maybe the mafia and the prostitute had caused us a problem, but I saw it was Nicholas, our ex-navy man in Vladivostok adorned in his full navy regalia and appearing to be the typical Russian naval officer. I burst out smiling and was very happy to see him, a fine person.

We had a great time with lots of laughs even though he was very difficult to understand. The businessman with him, whose name I can't remember, was engaged in the privatization of a $3 million business. Nicholas thought it would be great if I invested in the business, but he knew it was impossible as we were leaving so soon.

Nicholas brought Andy and me horizontal-striped tank shirts Russian sailors wore aboard ship. He also brought along some kopecks and rubles as mementos of our trip. He also gave me an epaulet with three stars on it and a small submarine. He was very proud of this, and so was I, although I was a little shocked that I would be carrying home something that was representative of the Russian navy. His partner told me that the epaulet was a commander's epaulet. We had seen many three-star military people throughout Russia, and I wasn't sure if Nicholas had been an officer or an enlisted man. I felt that since he had been discharged from the navy but was working with the navy in banking, he perhaps wore the uniform as an attention getter and was very proud of his service in the navy.

Nicholas wanted me to call him from America and wanted me to come with my wife to visit him. I told him she was a beautiful woman whom I have missed very much on this trip.

I confess that I had missed Marie terribly on many occasions. I thought about our initial dates in Jacksonville and how radiant she was. She always seemed to appreciate that description, and I was sure she still remembered it. I still think of her as radiant and as the woman with whom I was still very much in love. I mention that because certain videos and photos Andy and I had taken would show a certain amount of affection we'd had for some of the cuties we had met during our great Russian adventure.

Our visit to Vladivostok was very nice, and while we probably saw it sufficiently, it would have been nice to stay another day.

We went to the airport, were let out by our driver, and had to find our way to the ticket counter and the correct gate. From the marquee, which listed flight numbers, and a few Russian translations to English, I was able to determine some of the basics, and with some help from a couple who spoke some English, we were pretty confident we were headed in the right direction.

The flight to Moscow was going to be roughly fifty-eight hundred miles. It appeared to be about the same distance as on the train since we had to fly north and then west to keep from flying over China. Relations between Russia and China weren't the best just then.

Leonid, a Russian engineer who worked for a shipping company, sat beside me. He told us the flight was over the northern part of Siberia, perhaps close to the northern seas, which would cut down the travel time, which I estimated to be about eleven hours. The trip took nine hours.

Leonid and I talked a lot about the old Soviet Union and Russia. If we had been talking during KGB days, I'm sure I would have been arrested; I had all the earmarks of a CIA agent with all my questions. Andy would certainly have accompanied me because of his interest in the Russian navy at Vladivostok. We would have ended up in Lubyanka Prison in the basement of KGB headquarters in Moscow.

Leonid thought that Andy and I had been very brave to take the train trip by ourselves. He was very concerned about our safety, and shortly before the plane arrived, even though I had told him Intourist was meeting us, he had the plane officials call ahead for Intourist to meet us at the plane stairway rather than in the airport.

We had a special man escort us into the terminal, and they retrieved my checked bag at a later date, which gave me some cause for concern as we had a great deal of difficulty finding my bag. But things worked out well, and Leonid contributed to my inquisitive mind about this mysterious part of the world and one I had been intrigued about for the previous three years.

Incidentally, Leonid liked the democratic system of the day. He had just been employed by a new company and was moving from Vladivostok to Moscow. He said he was part owner of his company. He liked the new system simply because he had great opportunities to do things. However, his feeling was not shared by most of the people we had encountered since they weren't faring that well and worried more about money than they did about the political system under which they lived.

I envied Andy, who slept very well during most of the trip while I was able to sleep only about fifteen minutes. I continued reading my book, *Red Phoenix*. I had already finished reading a very good novel, *Promises to Keep*, which dealt with the Kennedy assassination and all the Kennedy characters throughout, given to me by Ken Clark. I enjoyed the book as much as Ken said he had.

Moscow—Wednesday, July 21, 1993

We checked into the Intourist Hotel, where we had spent four nights in early July, and snagged a large room as a result of Andy's efforts.

Andy and I were very thirsty and hungry; Aeroflot's service was very poor. We had less than a half of what we should have had to drink during the nine-hour flight. Our meal was probably fair by Russian standards, but I ate it solely out of necessity.

We went to the No. 1 McDonald's, a few blocks from the hotel. We had hamburgers, and I ordered two vanilla shakes and french fries. I got a second hamburger, but our original order ran 2,850 rubles, $2.85, fairly expensive in Moscow.

By the time we returned to the hotel, we had been up for twenty-two hours and were enduring a seven-hour time change. Andy was still going strong and didn't believe we had been up for that long, but the scoundrel also would probably not admit that he had slept for at least four hours, which was very close to a full night's sleep for me.

Andy and I had a few objectives on our return to Moscow, those that we hadn't been able to do because of our hurried departure. We had planned to visit the site of the American embassy and Gorky Park and to ride the metro, the largest subway system in the world. We also needed to buy a few gifts to take home.

We headed for one of the many tunnels under street intersections—numerous in Moscow—where entrepreneurs sell many different items.

We had planned to look at matryoshka dolls, the ones that stack inside each other; Marie had asked me to bring five back. Not knowing how to judge their quality, and not being fond of them myself, that was going to be an undertaking. We visited one tunnel and headed for Red Square. Andy was approached by an entrepreneurial guide named Nina; she sold her tour services for $5 an hour. Since someone else had mentioned Arbat Street as a good shopping area and Nina's services were low cost, we decided to use her for a couple of hours.

She discovered that several stores weren't open until 11:00 a.m. Under the state store system, they opened at ten, but evidently, opening at ten didn't prove profitable, so many started opening at eleven and staying open later. She suggested she take us on the metro to other areas. We thought that was a good plan since it would accomplish part of our day's objectives.

The metro was a thing of beauty, done in marble, a magnificent architectural spectacle when compared with subway systems in general. We saw quite a few stations along the way and were pleased that we did. We went into many shops, finally buying five matryoshkas.

The shopping routine was unmerciful in most stores. We were running short of rubles, and in more than one store, we had to convert dollars into rubles. For each transaction, we had to go to the purchase counter, get the amount of the items written down, take the bill to a cashier, pay, and return to the counter to retrieve the merchandise. However, the system kept many Russians employed. That I was sure would change dramatically with privatization and the profit motive.

We rode a boat on the Moscow River, and we walked a few blocks through a park and passed the Kremlin, taking pictures along the way. The Kremlin was highlighted with gold-domed minarets, onion tops as many of us say in the United States, which are symbols of the Kremlin and even Turkish architecture. We complimented Nina on the park next to the Kremlin having its grass cut. She indicated that they like all the parks to be very natural. Maybe that was the reason for all the unkempt parks we had seen. A Snapper representative could have made a killing in Russia if he was able to change the culture in this regard.

We walked through a park that had many homeless people in it. Nina pointed out that such homelessness didn't exist until perestroika came into existence with the new democracy in Russia. I told her that we had the same situation in America with many homeless and poor people, but that we all had the opportunity to capitalize on our freedom as she was doing.

I remember talking to a young woman from Vladivostok who had helped me arrange a telephone call home. She asked me if I thought Russia was in bad shape. I asked her if she meant buildings and roads. She said yes, and when I answered yes, I regretted that because her face dropped; she was disappointed. I told her that things were going to get much better in Russia in the future and that she would see buildings and many other things looking much better. That was the only time, I believe, that I unfortunately communicated something to a Russian that made him or her feel badly about Russia.

Nina lived in an apartment complex. Through some devious means that she explained but that I didn't understand completely, she had arranged for her husband to keep the apartment in which her deceased mother and father had lived. Evidently, such somewhat dishonest dealings went on throughout Russia because apartments were scarce. I meant to ask her the rent but failed to do so. She also said she had been without hot water for four months. She heated water in a pan daily for bathing. I remembered my feet being knocked out from under me in Ekaterinburg when I took that Siberian shower.

Nina pointed out Moscow University, a beautiful, tall structure, and Gorky Park. She kept us from going into Gorky Park, which I had read about being a place of intrigue with CIA and KGB agents and spies having so many clandestine meetings there. She said there was really nothing to see there.

I talked to Nina about religion in Russia. She confirmed what we had already learned—not many people, particularly the young, go to church. In only one case had I heard anyone say what her, in this case, specifics were related to religion. In Ulan Ude, Svetlana said she didn't go to church. "I do not believe in God. I am an atheist." Andy, a good Christian Southern Baptist, made a short attempt to convert her. All the evangelists and missionaries in Russia have their work cut out for them in creating a religious desire in a people whose parents and even grandparents had lived under a totalitarian, atheistic regime for more than seventy years. We know many dedicated people were doing this job today and were making progress, but they have one hundred and fifty million people minus a few to go.

Nina is a very nice person, very much like us, and was very talkative about her situation. She, like almost all Russian women, didn't drive and seemingly had no desire to do so. She said it was complicated. Andy and I agreed that we'd seen no more than ten women driving in Russia. In addition to so few cars being available, it was probably due to the culture and the desire of husbands to have the cars since there were so few. Andy and I discussed taking cars away from Betty and Marie when we got home if our culture would allow that.

We talked with Nina about salaries, and she said an Intourist staffer made 12,000 rubles monthly. Thinking I must have misunderstood her, she repeated it. That was only $12 a month. She said that Intourist people would buy tickets to the Bolshoi Theater for $1 and resell them for $30. That was part of the corrupt practices existing in the Soviet Union. I would have thought that the Communist society was so disciplined that things of that nature didn't occur, but that was not true at all.

Nina took us back to the subway and asked if we wanted to see the most beautiful station in the city, and we said yes. She took us down, down, down on tremendously long escalators. The metro system was so huge, with so many routes throughout the city, that there must have been at least three or four levels. I had the feeling that we were one thousand feet down. These subway stations had beautiful artwork in mosaics that were tributes to the revolution and the people and parties involved; they will probably last centuries. Russia probably had more marble than all the other countries in the world put together from the appearance of things; it was widely used even in low-cost buildings. The subway system probably handled more people in one day than all the subway systems in America together handle in one day—something more than twelve million, with another eight million on buses, trams, and other means of public transportation.

Andy and I thought that no one could have conceived what such a subway system would have cost. Under the Communist system as I understood it, they didn't know what their budget deficits were as recently as three years earlier. They were probably like someone who spends money with no regard until bankruptcy looms. That may be an overly simplistic view of the financial situation in Russia by someone not totally qualified to do so, but at least I feel free to make assumptions since I had a tremendous interest in the system.

We left the metro and saw the Metropole Hotel and large government buildings where the five-year plans were made many years ago; they never worked. We saw the KGB headquarters, which contained the infamous Lubyanka Prison, renowned as one of the worst prisons in the world during the days of the notorious KGB. When we were there, the KGB had become the Department or Division of Safety. We also saw the Bolshoi Theater, and we wished we'd seen the ballet, but someone had said it was not in season and tickets were somewhat difficult to get anyway.

Andy and I returned to the hotel and retrieved our baggage. The cost for storing our four bags was $7.20, an amount I considered unjust and an example of profiteering at the expense of those who didn't understand by people who didn't face competition.

We arrived at the railroad station with Intourist help; someone met us there to take us to the train and check us in. We checked into a nice compartment with made-up beds, which we'd had to do ourselves on other trains, and we felt comfortable. We'd had some dread of the Odessa trip, having heard certain things about it. But locking ourselves in with the famous "Andy Locking Utilitarian Device," we felt safe and had a nice rest for the night.

We didn't meet anyone on the train; everyone kept to their rooms, the only thing about that trip that was unusual. On almost all other trips, we had conversed with others and made friends.

At lunch, a man named Vladimena, who spoke only Russian, accompanied by his associate, Alec, who spoke reasonable English, suggested we eat beside them in the dining car. We ate soup with noodles and roasted or baked chicken, the same menu we'd had the night before. Our breakfast was instant coffee, even though Andy was not usually a coffee drinker, accompanied by peanut butter crackers and three Oreos each. Andy bought three boiled eggs at a stop and very graciously gave me two. We'd had boiled eggs for breakfast, and on quite a few occasions, we ate eggs that had been fried but without any grease and very little taste. On occasion, we had real fried eggs, which tasted very good. If only they had been accompanied by toast or bread other than the very flat, tasteless bread that we had been served throughout what was a Communist empire.

The train trip through Russia to Ukraine was through a broad expanse of flat country. We saw vast wheat fields in Ukraine, the breadbasket of the Soviet Union. The countryside was not especially beautiful, but our vision was obscured by trees along the tracks, and our window didn't give us a good perspective. I recalled looking out the window of our train in Mongolia and saw its rear coming around a mountain. The scenery was picturesque, but it couldn't have been enjoyed adequately just looking out the window. That may be the reason I hadn't considered Siberia to be especially beautiful, even though certain parts had low mountains and could be described as pretty.

We were surprised at how cold it was—the temperature must have been about forty-five. We were traveling south; Odessa was about eight hundred miles south of Moscow, but it was still far enough north to be on about the same parallel with the northern border of Maine or even a couple of hundred miles north of Montreal. Another difference in Ukraine was the lack of villages alongside the tracks, which we had seen and had found interesting in Siberia.

Arriving in Odessa, we were met by the ever-faithful Intourist and taken to the hotel, where we checked in to our $242 room for one night. The price included our pickup at the train station and a return there after our stay, which we extended for two days and paid only $60 for.

Odessa, Ukraine—Saturday, July 24, 1993

Odessa, a major port on the Black Sea, is a city of approximately 1.3 million. It had become part of Russia at the end of World War I and was much the same as Russia itself as far as customs and business went. We discovered again that the central system wasn't providing very warm water; my shower wasn't very comfortable. The shower was completely open, and the sink and commode received a bath at the same time as my body. Our tour guide (more about her shortly) said she had been without hot water for four months; just like Nina in Moscow, she heated water in a pan for bathing.

Our official schedule ended after our first night's stay in the Hotel Chernoe More. From that point on, we would be on our own. We planned to travel from Odessa to Istanbul across the Black Sea, as there were no railroads going through Romania and Bulgaria to Istanbul. Our top priority was securing transportation to Istanbul, and we found a small passenger ship leaving for Istanbul on Monday and arriving there on Wednesday.

Ella, our tour guide, secured our tickets. While they were being written, the ticket agent told her this wasn't the kind of transportation Americans were accustomed to and it could be dangerous. We changed our minds. We found out we could fly on a commuter airline on Monday for a total of $185. We went to the business office of the company, secured tickets, and started our tour of Odessa.

Our guide was accompanied by her driver, Igor, in a Mercedes, which were becoming much more prominent in the old Soviet Union. We went to the edge of the Black Sea and watched the ships. I realized I was probably wrong in thinking that the Russian naval fleet was being held in Odessa while Russia and Ukraine settled issues about who owned it. We discovered that the Russian fleet was in Sevastopol, a disappointment to Andy and me.

We visited a memorial to the Unknown Sailor in World War II. It had two monuments to the crew of two submarines; each of their names was inscribed on the monument. The Soviets were very thankful to the twenty-five million lost in World War II, though some say it was thirty million. They worked hard to keep the population loyal and have something for which they could be thankful since so many things had been so futile.

Ella pointed out the downtown building where Armand Hammer, deceased CEO of Occidental Petroleum, had been born. Not realizing before that he had been born in the Soviet Union, I then understood his many years of close association with the Soviet heads of state.

Ella was a very vivacious, intelligent, and well-educated tour guide. She was a civil engineer but not engaged in that profession because she didn't like it. She had spent five weeks in the northern California area of St. Cloud with a man she had met in Ukraine whom she said had been calling her several times a week trying to get her to move to the United States. Her return to Odessa was only a couple of weeks before our arrival.

Ella made arrangements for us to visit the Odessa Ballet and Opera House on Saturday evening. She described it as one of the most beautiful in the world on the inside; the outside was being refurbished. We saw *Don Quixote*, and it was extremely well done. The Soviets have paid strict attention to this kind of culture and value it very highly, and on the three occasions we'd visited ballets and other entertainment, the houses were filled.

After the ballet, we walked Ella about a half mile to her bus stop and walked back to our hotel. Ella suggested that we shouldn't speak English loudly on the very dark, tree-lined streets during the walk back to our hotel, which was probably a mile and a half.

Ella suggested that she meet us on Sunday at about 11:00 a.m. and show us around the city. This was done without any prearrangement for fees, and upon meeting her, we felt she evidently hadn't planned to charge us. Her beautiful eight-year-old daughter accompanied her, and they looked elegant. Yana was also very intelligent; her mother was teaching her English, and when we asked her name, she spoke very clear English, in fact somewhat better than her mother did. Ella and Yana were sophisticated and had tremendous personalities.

We walked through a park and saw art on exhibition and a movie being made. The park had been mowed; when we commented on that, Ella said Americans cut grass all the time, which is of course true. It appeared that it may not have been a lack of funds that caused parks to be overgrown; it may have been the way they liked it.

Yana and Andy took a four-wheel bicycle ride, and later, because Andy's shoes were slipping off the pedals, he sat in the middle while Yana and Ella handled the pedaling. Slick Andy. I became very jealous, borrowed his video, accused him of falling in love, and let him know that I had more pictures I'd use back in Atlanta. Who knew? Perhaps I'd end up owning two jewelry stores.

In the afternoon, Ella had some difficulty making up her mind where to eat. We walked to a nice restaurant, and she and Yana ordered for us. We had a variety of salads unlike any we'd had so far. One of our problems had been not knowing what to order on so many occasions.

We spoke at length with Ella. Her personal life was a little cloudy at the time. After getting on fairly common ground with her, she indicated that she was in love with the man in California, who was her senior by twenty-one years. She had attempted to get visas for her family to move to America, but it hadn't been possible. She knew that if she married the man, she would have an automatic entry to America, but she didn't want to leave her mother and father, who were fifty-one and fifty-six and in bad health.

She explained that her husband wasn't really her husband; they had not married. I didn't ask her why she referred to him in that manner. She explained that another man was her daughter's father, but he paid absolutely no attention to her. I was amazed that a man could ignore such a sweet little girl.

She indicated that her "husband" cried a lot, thinking he was going to lose her to the man in California. She was close to tears, so I talked fast to keep her from crying.

Concerning her parents' health, we talked about longevity in the Soviet Union, which is sixty-four for men and seventy-five for women. She mentioned that the health care system was bad; it didn't have many needed medicines, and the men drank a lot of vodka. She thought that was because they didn't have promising futures to look forward to. We had certainly witnessed the drinking.

In the afternoon, when we were leaving Ella, we saw a man in the park whom we thought was dead. Later, he was picked up by head and feet and carried into an apartment. Ella said he was drunk. She became almost tearful again when talking about the plight of the people in her country.

She pointed out that very few cars were on the streets as gasoline was in very short supply and very expensive. I asked her about the schools and how the children felt about Lenin, remembering what someone had said about "Grandpa" Lenin. She said that one day her daughter had come home from school very excited and said that she loved Grandpa Lenin more than anyone else in the world. She also said that she and Yana had worn red stars while in school. It seemed that throughout the old Soviet Union, the leaders did things to keep the people pumped up with war memorials and other things that would strengthen their loyalty and love for what they called their motherland. It was a very nice day; Andy and I felt close to someone in a country that faced a very bleak future for many years to come.

Monday was to be a trying day for the flight to Istanbul. We left the hotel about 9:00 a.m. and arrived at the airport, having some doubt about where our flight would depart. The person who met us at the airport after Intourist let us off was puzzled; he indicated there was no such airline. He moved around and asked questions, and we waited for some time. I decided to give him one more hour and then take some other action, as there was a possibility that if we missed that flight, we'd miss our flight from Istanbul to Atlanta.

At ten, I rounded up the guy who had a serious failure to communicate. He found someone who spoke English, and we learned that our flight was out of Kiev; he didn't know anything about the airline we were supposed to fly, and he left us hanging. I convinced the man to call the airline. He did so and came back quickly, satisfying us that the flight would depart from exactly where we were.

The plane was larger than expected—we were among about forty passengers—and we flew across the Black Sea, evidently fairly close to Romania and Bulgaria, but the clouds prevented us from spotting the earth.

Istanbul, Turkey—Monday Evening, July 26, 1993

We hired a person from customs to take us to the hotel, which he had difficulty locating in the heavy traffic. We checked into the old Hotel Konak and felt very good about the hustle and bustle we were seeing once again.

I was excited to be in Istanbul, which was so different from where we had spent the last forty-plus days. It was the same feeling I'd had when, after visiting four Communist countries, we crossed the Baltic Sea into very prosperous Finland.

Turkey is a country of approximately fifty-five million, eleven million of whom are in Istanbul. Istanbul had always been very interesting to me. Knowing that the Straits of Bosporus and the Dardanelles were the only connection between the Black Sea and the Mediterranean, I'd always wondered about how quickly we could bottle up the Soviet fleet in the Black Sea if we ever went to war with Russia.

Most of Istanbul is in Europe; a small part of the city is across the Bosporus in Asia. It's a very modern, prosperous city; we saw many new buildings and all the material things that those in the capitalist world would ever desire. The temperature was quite a bit warmer, perhaps in the eighties, which was nice for a change, but it was much cooler than Atlanta.

Andy and I took a stroll from the hotel. We were hungry, as we'd had only a small breakfast. I'd had two eggs fried in a dry pan, and I believe Andy had eaten an omelet. The streets were full of vegetable stands with such magnificent fruit, including bananas, peaches, apples— anything we wanted. We bought some delicious peaches and pears.

We returned to our hotel for lunch, and we had a very good filet smothered in a sauce and with white bread. In my opinion, it was the best meal we'd had since leaving Atlanta.

The next day, we took an all-day tour that include seeing the Bosporus, lunch, and a visit to the highest point of the city, overlooking the Bosporus and the Sea of Marmara, complemented by a visit to a very beautiful palace that had been built between 1861 and 1865 called the Beylerbeyi. It was the summer residence of Ottoman sultans.

In the evening, Andy and I took a long walk past many small cafes along the street with very beautiful food, such as large rolls of beef that were being cut and sliced, ears of corn being roasted and boiled—you name it, it was all available. I wanted to eat it all. We decided, believe it or not, to stop at McDonald's, and that too was very good.

The next day, the fifty-first day of our trip, we arranged for a tour and visited St. Sophia Mosque built between 535 and 537. St. Sophia had four minarets and was very much the picture of Turkey. The visit to this mosque was followed by a visit to the Blue Mosque, which had been built in the seventeenth century and is the only mosque in the world with six minarets. Only Mecca in Saudi Arabia had more minarets—seven.

We had left our shoes at the door, and as we left, I discovered my shoes were missing and those that had been beside mine when I entered the mosque were there. I assumed correctly that someone had switched shoes. We waited around a few minutes, but no one returned. I put the shoes on and gave my name to the proper people so I could be contacted if someone came back. The shoes were about the same size as mine. My shoes had become so dirty that even though they were nicer than my newly acquired shoes, I wasn't particularly disturbed by the loss.

Leaving the Blue Mosque reminded me of a very interesting thing on our first day of tour, a visit to the Egyptian spice market that had been established hundreds of years ago. We saw many spices but also jewelry, fruit, fish, and just about everything else. Turkey was a land of plenty and a good example of how people with incentive could prosper.

During the tour, Andy told me about a family from Virginia, Penke Davidson and her two children, Kevin and April. Penke was a native of Turkey and had married an American. When she said she was from Lynchburg, Virginia, I told her it was my home town. She couldn't believe it. Andy and I established a nice friendship with this family and were on the same flight from Istanbul to Frankfurt. I promised to call them when in Lynchburg. April, who was about eight, promised me a date.

After lunch, we visited the Topkapi Palace. Of particular interest was the spoon diamond, an eighty-six-carat diamond with forty-six brilliants encircling it. We also saw the world's largest uncut emerald, which I think was in the eighty-carat range.

That concluded a good two-day tour, and even though our time in Istanbul was limited, we saw the city, met all kinds of people, and have conversations with our tour guides. I was especially interested in talking with Ahmet about the situation in Turkey, the relationship with Russia, the importance of the Bosporus to Russia, and other items about which I had read and knew about from years past. He indicated there were serious terrorist problems in Turkey and worries about oil being transported out of the southern republics of the old Soviet Union through the Bosporus. They were scared to death their beautiful part of the world could be ruined. The Bosporus was lined with magnificent palms, houses, and boats along its shores and was a place I would remember as a place of wealth, brilliance, and the very best type living.

We returned to the hotel and got a call from the person who had my shoes. They were very mad at me and blamed the whole thing on me. They requested that I pay $14 for a taxi to get the shoes back to them, which I refused to do since they had taken my shoes and left theirs shoes. They called back a few minutes later and said they were bringing the shoes. Upon their arrival in the lobby, they were very angry, wanting the shoes I was wearing, but I didn't see my shoes. I asked about them, and they said they would give me my shoes if I paid then $2.50 for the taxi fare. I said I wasn't going to do that and headed for the elevator. They were very belligerent, and I thought I might have to engage in physical action before it was all over. I decided I wasn't being very wise, since my shoes were more valuable returned. I said I'd pay the $2.50. They went outside and got a man of about seventy-five, who appeared to be somewhat senile, and he came in with my shoes. I assumed that when he took the shoes, he hadn't been able to determine they weren't his.

The great puzzle was that they had blamed me. I told the very nice man at the hotel cashier stand, who was probably part owner of the hotel, that I had paid up only for the sake of Turkish-American relations. He pointed out that those people weren't Turks but Israelis. I then understood. We smiled, and I left with my shoes.

Andy and I decided we would walk, not knowing what we would eat, but we came across a place that offered shishkabobs roasted in a wood-fired oven. We took a look, and the people sold us on staying. The place had no roof, but the weather was nice. We wanted one skewer, but they furnished us with at least two and a good salad. The waitress removed the skewered vegetables and meat and placed them in pita bread; we thoroughly enjoyed it.

That ended the day. I was very excited about going home the next day.

Back to Atlanta—Thursday, July 29, 1993

Our flight left at 8:05 a.m. for Frankfurt. We were served a great breakfast, about ten times superior to Aeroflot fare; we had much to eat and drink on our flight.

Our very good looking stewardess on the flight was most pleasant. I was surprised to learn that she was from Warsaw, since she was so blond and spoke English almost without an accent. For some reason, I thought she could have been from Atlanta. I discovered that she flew from Frankfurt to Warsaw. She was surprised when I said thank you in Polish, "Genquia." She asked how I knew that. I told her about being in Warsaw, and she was delighted. I told her that I hoped she was being paid Atlanta Delta rates, but she said she was paid Warsaw rates. When I asked her how she felt about the new system of democracy, she registered her indifference with a shrug, the response we had received from most people in the ex-Communist countries we had visited.

We learned that our flight was going to take slightly longer than expected—about nine hours or more, probably because of headwinds, and that we would arrive in Atlanta about an hour late.

We had a wonderful lunch of a filet of beef accompanied by a good salad and other delicious things. I wanted to refrain from eating so much so that I would be hungry by the time we got to Atlanta. I could bet that Marie would be very disappointed if my appetite was completely satisfied when arriving home. I thought we would go out to eat, but

I thought she wanted to cook something, knowing that I had been somewhat hungry for a long time. I was excited about seeing Marie and hugging her after our long separation.

To paraphrase the young female college graduate on the Dow Chemical commercials that ran extensively for some time, I close this journal of our odyssey with, "I can't wait!"

Portugal, Spain, Morocco, and France

Date	City
May 1 (Sun)	Leave Atlanta 5:00 p.m. Delta #62; Arrive NY (Kennedy) 7:15 p.m. Leave NY 8:55 p.m. Delta #96; Arrive Lisbon 9:50 a.m.
May 2, 3 (Mon, Tues)	Lisbon—tour of city
May 4 (Wed)	Leave for Seville
May 5 (Thurs)	Seville
May 6 (Fri)	Cadiz
May 7 (Sat)	Gibraltar
May 8 (Sun)	Morocco
May 9 (Mon)	Morocco
May 10, 11, 12, 13	Costa del Sol, Malaga, Torremolinos, and traveling
May 14 (Sat)	Granada and Toledo—Parador de Granada?
May 15 (Sun)	Madrid
May 16 (Mon)	Madrid
May 17 (Tues)	Barcelona
May 18 (Wed)	Barcelona
May 19 (Thurs)	Toulouse
May 20 (Fri)	Bordeaux
May 21 (Sat)	Nantes

May 22 (Sun)	Cherbourg
May 23 (Mon)	Around Normandy area. Cherbourg, St. Michel, Utah, Omaha, Gold, and other landing beaches
May 24 (Tues)	Around Normandy area
May 25 (Wed)	Traveling toward Paris
May 27, 28, 29	Paris
May 30	Leave Paris Delta #21 12:10 p.m.; Arrive Atlanta 3:15 p.m.

Russian Trip

Time Zones of Cities Where Nights Were Spent in Hotels

If necessary to call a hotel in which Andy and I stayed, allow for the time difference based on the schedule below. For example, when it's 7:00 a.m. in Atlanta, it's 3:00 p.m. the same day in Moscow. Where departures and arrivals for trains, etc., are shown in the more detailed itinerary, military time is used.

Date in Hotel	Country and City	Time
	United States, Atlanta	7:00 a.m.
June 8, 9, 10	Poland, Warsaw	1:00 p.m.
	Europejski Hotel; ph. 011-48-22-265-051	
June 11	Lithuania, Vilnius	2:00 p.m.
	Hotel Lietuva; ph. 011-370-2-73-2215	
June 13	Latvia, Riga	2:00 p.m.
	Hotel Latvia: ph. 011-371-2-21-2525	
June 15	Estonia, Tallinn	2:00 p.m.
	Hotel Viru; ph. 011-372-2-65-2070	
June 16, 17, 18	Finland, Helsinki	2:00 p.m.
	Hotel Vaakuna; ph. 011-358-0-13-1181	
June 19–24	Russia, St. Petersburg	3:00 p.m.

	Hotel Pribaltiyskaya; ph. 011-7-812-356-5112	
June 24–27	Russia, Moscow	3:00 p.m.
	Hotel Intourist; ph. 011-7-095-203-4007	
June 30, July 1	Russia, Ekaterinburg	5:00 p.m.
	Hotel Oktyabrskaya	
July 3	Russia, Omsk	6:00 p.m.
	Hotel Turist	
July 6, 7	Russia, Irkutsk	8:00 p.m.
	Hotel Intourist; ph. 011-7-3952-91-3535	
July 10–12	Mongolia, Ulan Bator	8:00 p.m.
	Hotel Boyangel; ph. 011-976-28632	
July 14	Russia, Ulan Ude	8:00 p.m.
	Hotel Geser	
July 17–18	Russia, Khabarovsk	10:00 p.m.
	Hotel Intourist; ph. 011-7-421-2-33-7634	
July 19–20	Russia, Vladivostok	10:00 p.m.
	Hotel Vladivostok	

Headed back east for return trip

July 21	Russia, Moscow	3:00 p.m.
	Hotel Intourist; ph. 011-7-095-203-4007	
July 22–23	Ukraine, Odessa	3:00 p.m.
	Hotel Chernoe More; ph. 011-7-048-2-24-2024	
July 24–25	Ukraine, Kiev (Not definite)	3:00 p.m.
July 26–28	Turkey, Istanbul	2:00 p.m.
	Hotel Konak; ph. 011-90-1-248-4744	
July 29	Atlanta	

Hotel telephone numbers shown include 011 for international operator, then the country number, then the city number, and the local number. Just dial as shown.

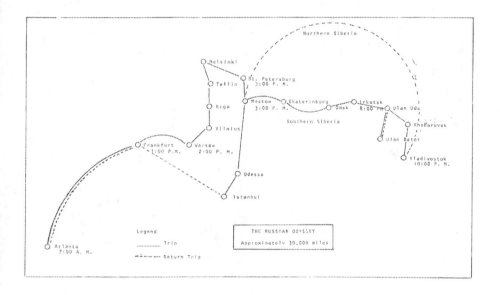

Printed in the United States
By Bookmasters